PSB HOAE Test Strategy

Winning Multiple Choice Strategies Health Occupations Aptitude Examination Exam

COMPLETE
TEST PREPARATION INC.
WWW.TEST-PREPARATION.CA

Copyright © 2013 by Brian Stocker. ALL RIGHTS RESERVED. No part of this book may be reproduced or transferred in any form or by any means, graphic, electronic, or mechanical, including photocopying, recording, web distribution, taping, or by any information storage retrieval system, without the written permission of the author.

Notice: Complete Test Preparation makes every reasonable effort to obtain from reliable sources accurate, complete, and timely information about the tests covered in this book. Nevertheless, changes can be made in the tests or the administration of the tests at any time and Complete Test Preparation makes no representation or warranty, either expressed or implied as the accuracy, timeliness, or completeness of the information contained in this book. Complete Test Preparation makes no representations or warranties of any kind, express or implied, about the completeness, accuracy, reliability, suitability or availability with respect to the information contained in this document for any purpose. Any reliance you place on such information is therefore strictly at your own risk.

The author(s) shall not be liable for any loss incurred as a consequence of the use and application, directly or indirectly, of any information presented in this work. Sold with the understanding, the author is not engaged in rendering professional services or advice. If advice or expert assistance is required, the services of a competent professional should be sought.

The company, product and service names used in this publication are for identification purposes only. All trademarks and registered trademarks are the property of their respective owners. Complete Test Preparation is not affiliated with any educational institution.

We strongly recommend that students check with exam providers for up-to-date information regarding test content.

ISBN-13: 9781772451832

Version 5 March 2019

Published by
Complete Test Preparation Inc.
Victoria BC Canada
Visit us on the web at https://www.test-preparation.ca
Printed in the USA

The PSB Health Occupations Aptitude Exam is administered by the Psychological Services Bureau, who are not involved in the production of this book and do not endorse this product.

About Complete Test Preparation Inc.

The Complete Test Preparation Team has been publishing high quality study materials since 2005. Over one million students visit our websites every year, and thousands of students, teachers and parents all over the world (over 100 countries) have purchased our teaching materials, curriculum, study guides and practice tests.

Complete Test Preparation is committed to providing students with the best study materials and practice tests available on the market. Members of our team combine years of teaching experience, with experienced writers and editors, all with advanced degrees.

Feedback

We welcome your feedback. Email us at feedback@test-preparation.ca with your comments and suggestions. We carefully review all suggestions and often incorporate reader suggestions into upcoming versions. As a Print on Demand Publisher, we update our products frequently.

Contents

6 Getting Started with the PSB
Multiple Choice Strategy — 8

11 Multiple-Choice Quick Tips

14 Answering Multiple-Choice Step-by-Step

18 Multiple-Choice Strategy Practice Questions
Answers Key — 38

51 Basic Math Multiple-Choice Strategy
Math Multiple-Choice Strategy — 52
Answer Key — 63
Fraction Tips, Tricks and Shortcuts — 69
Decimal Tips, Tricks and Shortcuts — 73
Percent Tips, Tricks and Shortcuts — 74

77 Word Problem Multiple-Choice Strategy
Types of Word problems — 79
Practice Questions — 89
Answer Key — 92

96 How to Improve your Vocabulary
Meaning in Context — 101
The Top 100 Common Vocabulary — 115
Stem Words — 119
Stem Words Practice Questions — 129
Stem Words Practice Part II — 139
Most Common Prefix — 147
Prefix Questions — 150
Most Common Synonyms — 158
Synonym Practice Questions — 163
Word List 5 – Most Common Antonyms — 173
Antonym Practice Questions — 178

186 How to Prepare for a Test
The Strategy of Studying — 188

191 How to Take a Test
Reading the Instructions — 191
How to Take a Test - The Basics — 192
In the Test Room – What you MUST do! — 196
Common Test-Taking Mistakes — 201

https://www.facebook.com/CompleteTestPreparation/

https://www.youtube.com/user/MrTestPreparation

https://www.instagram.com/completetestpreparation/

https://www.pinterest.ca/brians6634/boards/

Getting Started with the PSB

CONGRATULATIONS! By deciding to take the Health Occupations Aptitude Examination (PSB or HOAE) you have taken the first step toward a great future! Of course, there is no point in taking this important examination unless you intend to do your best to earn the highest grade you possibly can. That means getting yourself organized and discovering the best approaches, methods and strategies to master the material. Yes, that will require real effort and dedication, but if you are willing to focus your energy and devote the study time necessary, before you know it you will be finished the exam with a great mark!

We know that taking on a new endeavour can be a scary, and it is easy to feel unsure of where to begin. That's where we come in. This guide is designed to help you improve your test-taking skills, show you a few tricks and increase your competency and confidence.

The PSB Exam

The PSB is composed of the following subject areas, Paragraph Comprehension, Basic Math, Algebra, Metric Conversion, Word Problems, Life Science (Biology, Ecology), Earth and Physical Science, Chemistry, Spelling and Vocabulary. Not all schools require all modules, so be sure to check with your school to make sure you are studying the right subjects! Since how well you score in each of these areas will determine whether or not you can be admitted, it is important to be prepared.

Test Strategy

This is a book about improving your score by using proven test strategies. This is different from other books such as a study guide, or a practice test. Even though we do provide lots of information to study and practice test questions, this book is about how to tackle multiple choice questions. But don't worry - that's not all! While you are learning different strategies for answering multiple choice questions, you can also practice your skill at answering reading comprehension test questions, which are part of your score on the PSB.

The other section of the PSB is basic math. We provide strategies for answering multiple choice math questions, plus tips, tricks and shortcuts that save you valuable time.

And finally, we include powerful vocabulary boosting techniques, with practice questions, to get your vocabulary up to speed for the exam.

So let's get started!

Multiple Choice Strategy

A Better Score Is Possible

Worried about that big exam coming up? Do you think you're just not a good test-taker, especially when it comes to standardized tests? The good news is that you're not alone. The bad news is that millions of people are left behind through objective testing, simply because they're not good test-takers - even though they may know the material. They don't know how to handle the format well or understand what's expected of them.

This is especially true of the multiple-choice test. Test-takers are given alot of support for taking essay-style tests. They're helped with skills such as grammar and spelling. However, little is offered for the multiple-choice exam. Even though thousands of people find multiple-choice to be the most challenging type of test. Here are some reasons that so many people have difficulties with multiple-choice:

The Broad Range. Because the questions are so short and quick, a lot of ground is covered in the test. Who's to know what to study with so much material covered?

Time Limits. Most standardized tests have time limits, which adds an extra layer of pressure.

Trickery. Many test-designers think that it is too easy to guess a multiple-choice question correctly, so they intentionally make the questions tricky.

Bluffing Not Allowed. With an essay test, you can try to bluff your way through it. Not so with multiple-choice. The answer is either right or wrong.

Difficult to Write. It's not easy for a test-writer to design a good multiple-choice test. Sometimes, they make them overly difficult.

Shuffled Content. Multiple-choice tests tend to throw the questions in at random, in no particular order. You could be answering a question about the 1700s and then about the 2004 Presidential election.

These challenges mean that students have to be familiar with a wider range of material than on other kinds of exams. You'll need to know specific vocabulary, rules, names, dates, etc.

There are, however, a few advantages to you, the test-taker, with a multiple-choice test. For instance, because there are more multiple-choice items on a test than other types, each question tends to have a lower point value. You can afford to miss a few and still be okay. Also, if you're doing a fill-in-the blank or essay test, you have to rely totally on memory for the answer. With a multiple-choice exam, you know that the correct answer is somewhere in the question. You just have to decide which one it is. Often, seeing the right answer will trigger your memory, and you'll recognize it instantly.

Keep in mind, though, the test-writer knows that one advantage of multiple-choice is the fact the answer is on the page. Therefore, many test-writers include what is called a "distracter." This is a possible answer that is designed to look like the correct answer, but which is actually wrong. We'll talk about this again later, but an example would be the question: "Who is known for posting 95 theses on a church wall?" Among the answers might be Martin Luther and Martin Luther King. Because the student vaguely remembers the name "Martin Luther" from the course materials, there's a chance that he'll select the incorrect "Martin Luther King."

Who Does Well On Multiple-Choice Exams?

With so many challenges working against you on the multiple-choice exam, what's the answer? Is there a way to improve your chances and your score? There is! The point of this book is not to discourage you, but to make you aware that there are strategies and tips that you can incorporate to raise your test score. Before we get into the specific strategies, let's take a general look at who does best on these types of tests.

Those who know the material. This should go without saying, but the thing that will most raise your test score will be if you know the material that's going to be covered. While the strategies we'll discuss later will help you even with questions you're unsure of, the best thing you can do is learn the rules, dates, names, and concepts that you'll be tested on.

Those who have a calm, cool demeanor when taking a test. Panicking can cause you to forget the information you think you know. Confidence goes a long way toward a better mark on multiple-choice.

Those who meditate or pray before the test. Don't laugh. It's a fact that people who meditate or pray, depending on their beliefs, enter a test room more confidently, and do better on the exam.

Those who operate on logic rather than instinct. Those who take a multiple-choice test based on instinct will be tempted to overlook the stated facts, and let emotion rule.

Those who have a system. Most of this book will deal with this, but you should not just guess randomly on questions you don't know. You must have a systematic strategy.

Multiple-Choice Quick Tips

Before looking at specific strategies in detail, lets first look at some general tips that you can use on any test and on multiple-choice questions in any subject. We will explore some of these in more detail later.

- **Finding Hints without Cheating** Pssst. There is a way to get hints about a question, even as you are taking the test—and it is completely legal. The key: Use the test itself to find clues about the answer. Here is how to do this. If you cannot answer a question, read the answers. If you find one that uses the language that your teacher or textbook used, there is a good chance that this is the right answer. That is because on complex topics, teachers and books tend to always use the same or similar language.
Another point: Look out for test questions which are like previous questions. Often, you will find the same information used in more than one question.

  Occasionally you will find the answer to one question contained in another question - be on the lookout for this type of situation and use it to your advantage.

- **Before you try eliminating wrong answers, try to solve the problem.** If you know for sure that you have answered the question correctly, then obviously there is no need to eliminate wrong choices. If you cannot solve it, then see how many choices you can eliminate. Now try solving it again, and see if one of the remaining choices comes close to your answer. Your chances of getting the answer right have now improved dramatically. Elimination is the most powerful strategy and we will discuss in more detail, as well as practice below.

- **Skip if you do not know.** If you simply do not know the answer and do not know how to get the answer, mark the question in the margin and come back if you have time.

- **Rule out answers that seem so general that they do not offer much information.** If an answer said, for example, "Columbus came to the West in the spring," it is probably not the right answer.

- **Use "all of the above" and "none of the above" to your advantage.** For "all of the above," you do not need to check all the choices - just two of them. If two of the answers are correct, then this probably means they are all correct, and you can select "all." (This, of course, is not always the case, especially if there is also an option for "A and B" or "C and D."). Similarly, with "all of the above" questions, you only have to find one wrong answer, and then you have eliminated two choices - one is the wrong answer, and the other is All of the Above.

- **Let "close" answers be your guide.** The clever test-writer often includes an answer that is almost the correct one, to throw you off. The clever test-taker, however, can use this to his advantage. If you see two options that are strangely similar, then chances are good that one of these is the correct choice. That means you can rule out the other answers—and thus improve your chances. For instance, if two choices are George Washington and George Washington Carver, among Abraham Lincoln and Thomas Edison, there is a good chance that one of the two Washingtons is right. More on this strategy below.

Watch Out For Trick Questions

In general, most questions are what they appear to be and over-analyzing is a pitfall to be avoided. However, most multiple-choice tests contain one or two trick questions for a variety of reasons. A trick question is one where the test-writer intentionally makes you think that the answer is easier than it really is. Test-writers include trick questions because so many people think that they have mastered the techniques of taking a test that they need not study the material. In only a very few cases will a test have more than a handful of trick questions. Often instructors will include trick questions, where you really have to know your stuff inside-out to answer it correctly. This separates the "A" students from the "B−" students, and the "A" students from the "A+" students.

The best way to beat the trick question is to read the question carefully and break it down into parts. Then break it down into individual words. For instance, if a question asks,

> "When a plane crashes on the border between the United States and Canada, where are the survivors buried?"

if you had looked at each word individually, you would have realized that the last word, "survivors," means that the test writer is talking about burying people who are still alive.

Before You Change That Answer ...

You are probably familiar with the concept by now: your first instinct is usually right. This is why so many people, when giving advice about tests, tell you that unless you are convinced that your first instinct was wrong, do not take a chance. Here, more people change a right answer to a wrong one, more often than a wrong one to a right one.

How to Handle This.

Let's take that advice a step further, though. Maybe you do not always have to leave your first answer, especially if you think there might be a reasonable chance that your second choice was right. Before you go changing the answer, though, go on and do a few questions and clear your thoughts of the problem question. After you have done a few more, go back and start from the beginning. Then see if the original answer is still the one that jumps out at you. If so, leave it. If your second thought now jumps out at you, then go ahead and change it. If both are equal in your mind, then leave it with your first hunch.

Answering Multiple-Choice Step-by-Step

HERE IS A TEST QUESTION:

Which of the following is a helpful tip for taking a multiple-choice test?

   a. Answering "B" for all questions.

   b. Eliminate all answers that you know cannot be true.

   c. Eliminate all answers that seem like they might be true.

   d. Cheat off your neighbor.

If you answered B, you are correct. Even if you are not positive about the answer, try to eliminate as many choices as possible. Think of it this way: If every item on your test has four possible answers, and if you guess on one of those four answers, you have a one-in-four chance (25%) of getting it right. This means you should get one question right for every four that you guess.

However, if you can get rid of two answers, then your chances improve to one-in-two chances, or 50%. That means you will get a correct answer for every two that you guess.

So much for an obvious tip for improving your multiple-choice score. There are many other tips that you may or may not have considered, which will give your grade a boost. Remember, though, that none of these tips are infallible. In fact, many test-writers know these tips and deliberately write questions that will confound your system. Usually, however, you will do better on the test if you put these tips into practice.

By familiarizing yourself with these tips, you increase your chances and who knows; you might just get a lucky break and increase your score by a few points!

Answering Step-by-Step

It might seem complicated and unnecessary to follow a formula for answering a multiple-choice question. After you have practiced this formula for a while, though, it will come naturally and will not take any time at all. Try to follow these steps below on each question.

Step 1. Cover up the answers while you read the question. See the material in your mind's eye and try to envision what the correct answer is before you expose the answers on the answer sheet.

Step 2. Uncover the responses.

Step 3. Eliminate or Estimate. Cross out every choice that you know is ridiculous, absurd or clearly wrong. Then work with the answers that remain.

Step 4. Watch for distracters. A distracter is an answer that looks similar to the correct answer, but is put there to trip you up. If you see two answers that are strikingly similar, the chances are good that one of them is correct. For instance, if you are asked the term for the distance around a square, and two of the responses are "periwinkle" and "perimeter," you can guess that one of these is probably correct, since the words look similar (both start with "peri-"). Guess one of these two and your chances of correctly selecting "perimeter" are 50/50. More on this below.

Step 5. Check! If you see the answer that you saw in your mind, put a light check-mark by it and then see if any of the other choices are better. If not, mark that response as your answer.

Step 6. If all else fails, guess. If you cannot envision the correct response in your head, or figure it out by reading the passage, and if you are left totally clueless as to what the answer should be, guess.

The PSB does NOT penalize for wrong answers, so if you really do not know the answer, guessing is a good strategy.

There is a common myth that says choice "C" has a statistically greater chance of being correct. This may be true if your professor is making the test, however, most standardized tests are generated by computer and the choices are randomized. We do not recommend choosing "C" as a strategy.

That is a quick introduction to multiple-choice to get us warmed up. Next we move onto the strategies and practice test questions section. Each multiple-choice strategy is explained, followed by practice questions using the strategy. Opposite this page is a bubble sheet for answering.

ANSWER SHEET

	A	B	C	D	E			A	B	C	D	E
1	○	○	○	○	○		26	○	○	○	○	○
2	○	○	○	○	○		27	○	○	○	○	○
3	○	○	○	○	○		28	○	○	○	○	○
4	○	○	○	○	○		29	○	○	○	○	○
5	○	○	○	○	○		30	○	○	○	○	○
6	○	○	○	○	○		31	○	○	○	○	○
7	○	○	○	○	○		32	○	○	○	○	○
8	○	○	○	○	○		33	○	○	○	○	○
9	○	○	○	○	○		34	○	○	○	○	○
10	○	○	○	○	○		35	○	○	○	○	○
11	○	○	○	○	○		36	○	○	○	○	○
12	○	○	○	○	○		37	○	○	○	○	○
13	○	○	○	○	○		38	○	○	○	○	○
14	○	○	○	○	○		39	○	○	○	○	○
15	○	○	○	○	○		40	○	○	○	○	○
16	○	○	○	○	○		41	○	○	○	○	○
17	○	○	○	○	○		42	○	○	○	○	○
18	○	○	○	○	○		43	○	○	○	○	○
19	○	○	○	○	○		44	○	○	○	○	○
20	○	○	○	○	○		45	○	○	○	○	○
21	○	○	○	○	○		46	○	○	○	○	○
22	○	○	○	○	○		47	○	○	○	○	○
23	○	○	○	○	○		48	○	○	○	○	○
24	○	○	○	○	○		49	○	○	○	○	○
25	○	○	○	○	○		50	○	○	○	○	○

Multiple-Choice Strategy Practice Questions

THE FOLLOWING ARE DETAILED STRATEGIES FOR ANSWERING MULTIPLE-CHOICE QUESTIONS WITH PRACTICE QUESTIONS FOR EACH STRATEGY.

Answers appear following this section with a detailed explanation and discussion on each strategy and question, plus tips and analysis.

Strategy 1 - Locate Keywords

For every question, figure out exactly what the question is asking by locating key words that are in the question. Underline the keywords to clarify your thoughts and keep on track.

Directions: Read the passage below, and answer the questions using this strategy.

Free-range is a method of farming where domesticated animals roam freely, or relatively freely, rather than being kept in a pen or cage. Free-range can mean two different things depending on who you talk to. One definition, when talking to a farmer, is a technical description of a farming method. You may have seen free-range or free-run eggs in the supermarket. This is a consumer oriented definition. There are numerous benefits to farmers who practice free-range farming. Certification as a free-range producer allows farmers to charge higher prices and reduce feed costs. That's not all - free-range methods also improve the general health of animals, which produces a higher-quality product. In addition, free-range farming allows multiple crops on the same land - another significant savings for farmers. Free-range certification is different from organic certification.

1. The free-range method of farming

a. Uses a minimum amount of fencing to give animals more room.

b. Can refer to two different things.

c. Is always a very humane method.

d. Only allows for one crop at a time.

2. Free-range farming is practiced

a. To obtain free-range certification.

b. To lower the cost of feeding animals.

c. To produce higher quality product.

d. All of the above.

3. Free-range farming:

a. Can mean either farmer described or consumer described methods.

b. Is becoming much more popular ir

c. Has many limits and causes prices

d. Is only done to make the animals I healthier.

4. Free-range certification is most impo because:

a. Free-range livestock are less expen

b. The price of the product is higher.

c. Both A and B

d. The animals are kept in smaller enclosures, so more can be produced.

Strategy 2 - Watch Negatives

For every question, no matter what type, look for negatives. These can include never, not, and others that will completely change what is being asked.

Directions: Read the passage below, and answer the questions using this strategy.

Grizzly bears exhibit a common feature in nature, sexual dimorphism. This is where there are distinct difference in size or appearance between the sexes of an animal. Male grizzly bears, for example, generally weigh between 400 and 750 pounds, but can weight over 1,000 pounds. Females grizzlies are smaller, weighing 250 – 350 pounds, which is about 38% smaller. Female grizzlies stand about 3 feet at the shoulder, on all fours, and over 6 feet when standing upright. Males are bigger, generally standing 8 feet or more on their hind legs. Grizzlies in different geographical areas also show significant differences. For example, grizzlies from the Yukon River area in Northern Canada are 20% smaller.

5. Sexual dimorphism does not mean

   a. Male and female grizzly bears are the same size.

   b. All grizzly bears look the same and are the same size.

   c. Grizzly bears can be quite large, and weigh more than half a ton.

   d. All of the above

6. The size of a full-grown grizzly bear is never

   a. More than 500 pounds.

   b. Depends on the bear's sex.

   c. Determined simply by diet.

   d. Less than 8 feet tall.

7. Grizzly bears from the area of the Yukon River do not

   a. Get as big as most other grizzly bears do

   b. Get the rich and varied food supply needed

   c. Need the same nutrients as other grizzly bears

   d. Get less than 7 feet tall, and weigh close to half of a ton

Strategy 3 - Read the Stem Completely

For every question, no matter what type, read the information in the stem and then try to determine the correct answer before you look at the different answers.

Directions: Read the passage below, and answer the questions using this strategy.

Brown bears and grizzly bears are generally considered separate species, although technically, both are classified as Ursus Arctos. Brown bears live in coastal areas of North America where salmon is the primary food source. Bears found inland and in northern habitats are called 'grizzlies.' A sub species of Brown bears found on Kodiak Island, Alaska, have different shaped skulls due to the remote region and independent development.

Black bear, which are smaller and more common, are also a sub species, Ursus Americanus. Black bears are found throughout North America.

8. Grizzly bears, brown bears, and Kodiak bears are all

    a. Arctas Ursinas

    b. Ursus Arctos

    c. Arctos Ursina

    d. Ursula Arctic

9. Kodiak brown bears are classified as a different subspecies because

    a. They are much larger than other brown bears

    b. Their diet is radically different from that of other brown bears

    c. They are not true brown bears but instead a mixture of bear species

    d. Of their genetics and head shape, as well as their physical isolation

10. The term grizzlies, when referring to the brown bear, is used mainly

    a. In eastern areas where the bear grows large

    b. Only in snowy areas where there are low year round temperatures

    c. In the northern and inland areas

    d. In areas where the bear has a silver appearance

11. The term brown bear is normally used

    a. When one of the main food sources is salmon

    b. When the bear is small

    c. When the bear is found inland

    d. When the bear has a light brown coat and is very large

Strategy 4 - Consider all the Choices Before Deciding

For every question, no matter what type, make sure to read every option before making your choice.

Directions: Read the passage below, and answer the questions using this strategy.

Polar bears and grizzlies are different species although there are rare cases of hybrids. Scientists have known the two species are compatible for some time and there are several cases of hybrids in zoos.

In 2006, in Canada's Northwest Territories, a hunter shot what he thought was a polar bear. This bear, however, was slightly different. Like most polar bears, its fur was thick and white, as one would expect of a polar bear. However the bear also had some characteristics of grizzlies, such as long claws, a humped back, and brown patches around its nose, eyes and back.

This odd combination of features from both species soon attracted attention of the Wildlife Genetics International in British Columbia, Canada, which confirmed that this animal was a polar bear grizzly hybrid through DNA testing, and, the first hybrid found in the wild.

This bear appears to be the product of a polar bear mother and a grizzly bear father. Until 2006, there had been no documented cases of a grizzly polar bear hybrid found in the wild.

12. Which grizzly bear features did the hybrid bear have?

    a. Brown patches in certain areas

    b. Long claws

    c. A shallow face

    d. All of the above

13. The hybrid bear was the result of

   a. A male brown bear and a female grizzly.

   b. A female brown bear and a male grizzly bear.

   c. A female polar bear and a male grizzly bear.

   d. A male polar bear and a female grizzly.

14. The hybrid bear tested in this case was

   a. The first case ever known where two different bear species mated successfully.

   b. Genetically flawed and prone to many diseases and conditions.

   c. A fluke, and a mistake of nature which has never happened.

   d. The first proof of a wild bear hybrid species outside zoos.

15. Modern science

   a. Has proven that the cubs from two different species will not survive in almost every case.

   b. Has known for some time that these hybrid bears were possible.

   c. Completely understands how bear hybrids occur and why this happens in nature.

   d. Has studied hundreds of bear hybrids in an attempt to learn more.

Strategy 5 - Elimination

For every question, no matter what type, eliminating obviously incorrect answers narrows the possible choices. Elimination is probably the most powerful strategy for answering multiple-choice.

Directions: Read the passage below, and answer the questions using this strategy.

Peacocks have been admired throughout history for their beautiful plumage and train of the male peafowl, or peacock, with its characteristic eye pattern.

In Greek mythology, Hera, wife of Zuess, and queen of the Gods, placed the hundred eyes of the slain giant Argus on the tail of the peacock, her favorite bird.

The peacock's tail or train, is not actually the tail, but the elongated feathers of the upper tail. These beautiful green-bronze feathers, with the eye pattern, can be seen when the train is fanned out. The actual tail feathers of the peacock are short and grey-colored and can be seen from behind when the train is fanned in a courtship display.

The grey tail feathers can also be seen during molting season, when males drop the feathers in their train. The female peacock is duller compared to the spectacular male. The female is brown, with some green iridescence feathers on her neck.

16. The long colorful tail feathers of the peacock

    a. Are only present in the male of the species

    b. Are used by both sexes to warn off predators

    c. Are normally red and blue in color

    d. Are only present for a very short time each year

17. The differences between the male and female peacock are

    a. Size and weight

    b. Coloring and tail feather length

    c. The female does not ever leave the nest

    d. The male sits on and hatches the eggs

18. The term peacock actually refers to

    a. Both sexes of the pheasant family

    b. The eyes on the tail feathers of the bird

    c. Male peafowl

    d. Female peafowl

19. The gray tail feathers on the male peacock can be seen

    a. When the bird is startled

    b. Only when the bird is searching for food

    c. When the peacock lowers the tail feathers to the ground

    d. During molting season

Strategy 6 - Opposites

For every question, no matter what type, look at answers that are opposites. When two answers are opposites, the odds increase that one of them is the correct answer.

Directions: Read the passage below, and answer the questions using this strategy.

Smallpox is a highly infectious disease unique to humans, caused by two virus, Variola Major and Minor. The Latin name for smallpox is Variola or Variola Vera, which means spotted.

In 1980, the World Health Organization certified that Smallpox had been eradicated. Smallpox is sometimes confused with Chicken Pox, however, they are different virus.

The smallpox virus lives in the small blood vessels in the mouth, throat and skin. This gives a distinct rash in these areas, which turn into blisters. After being exposed to the Smallpox virus, symptoms do not appear for 12 to 17 days.

Variola Major is much more serious virus, with a mortality rate of 30 – 35%. Variola Minor is milder, with a mortality rate of only 1%. Variola Minor has several common names, including, alastrim, cottonpox, milkpox, whitepox, and Cuban itch.

Variola Major causes several long-term complications such as scars, commonly on the face, which occurs in about 65 – 85% of the survivors. Other complications, including blindness and deformities from arthritis and other complications are much less common, about 2 – 5%.

20. Smallpox

    a. Effects all mammals, including humans

    b. Is caused by a bacteria from contact with dead flesh

    c. Was called the great pox during the fifteenth century

    d. Only affects humans, although other species can carry and transmit the virus

21. Smallpox caused by Variola major has a

    a. Thirty to thirty five percent survival rate

    b. Sixty percent mortality rate

    c. Thirty to thirty five percent mortality rate

    d. Sixty percent survival rate

22. Smallpox caused by Variola minor is

    a. Much more severe, with more pox and scarring

    b. Much less severe, with fewer pox and less scarring

    c. Characterized because there are no pox

    d. So minor that no treatment or medical attention is needed

23. Smallpox can be fatal

  a. Between thirty and thirty five percent of those who catch the virus, depending on the type

  b. Between thirty and sixty five percent of those who catch the virus, depending on the type

  c. When no medical treatment is available

  d. Only in developing countries where medical care is poor

Strategy 7 - Look for Differences

For every question, no matter what type, look at the two choices that seem to be correct and then examine the differences. Refer to the stem to determine the best answer.

Directions: Read the passage below, and answer the questions using this strategy.

Lightning is one of the most amazing natural phenomena. A popular belief is that lightning cannot strike twice in the same place. This however, is not true - lightning does strike in the same place frequently.

Lightning is an electrical discharge between clouds and the ground, or between two clouds. It is often accompanied with thunder during thunderstorms, dust storms and volcanic eruptions. Every year, there are an estimated 16 million lightning storms worldwide.

Bolts of lightning travel at speeds of 130,000 miles per hour and contain a billion volts of electricity. Lightning bolts can reach temperatures of 54,000° F. This is hot enough to turn sand, some soils or even rock into hollow glass channels, called fulgurites. Fulgurites extend far below the surface.

Lightning is such a common feature of the natural world, there is even a classification for the fear of lightning and thunder, called astraphobia.

Clouds of volcanic ash, as well as dust storms and forest fires can generate enough static electricity to produce lightning.

Scientists do not understand the process of lightning formation, and this is a matter for debate. Scientists have studied causes of lightning, such as wind, humidity, friction, atmospheric pressure, solar winds and accumulation of charged solar particles. Many scientists believe that ice inside clouds is important in causing lightning.

24. Astraphobia is

    a. Fear of thunder

    b. Fear of thunder and lightning

    c. Fear of lightning

    d. None of the above

25. Lightning occurs

    a. Only in thunderstorms

    b. In thunderstorms and dust storms

    c. In thunderstorms, volcanic eruptions and dust storms

    d. In the upper atmosphere

26. Fulgurites are

    a. Made of silica

    b. Made of glass

    c. Made of sand, soil and rock turned into glass

    d. Made of silica and glass

Strategy 8 - Context clues

Look at the sentences and the context to determine the best option. Sometimes, the answer may be located right in the passage or question.

Directions: Read the passage below, and answer the questions using this strategy.

Venus is one of the four solar terrestrial planets, or rocky bodies that orbit the sun. Planets are defined as a celestial body moving in an elliptical orbit around a star. Venus is about the same size as Earth. Venus' diameter (12,104 km) is only 650 km. less than Earth's, (12,742 km.) and its mass is 81.5% of Earth's. The Venusian atmosphere is a dense mixture of carbon dioxide with some nitrogen.

Venus orbits the sun every 224.7 days, and is the second-closest planet to the Sun.

Venus, as the second brightest star in the sky, after the moon, reaches an apparent magnitude of −4.6, was named after Venus, the goddess of love and beauty by the Romans. The Romans named all the brightest stars after their Gods and Goddesses. Venus is often called the Morning, or Evening Star. Venus reaches its maximum brightness before sunrise and after sunset

Venus is an inferior planet from Earth, meaning that it is closer to the sun: its elongation reaches a maximum of 47.8°.

27. Apparent magnitude is

    a. A measure of darkness

    b. A measure of brightness

    c. The distance from the moon

    d. The distance from the earth

28. The elongation of a planet is

    a. The angular distance from the sun, as seen from earth.

    b. The distance from the sun

    c. The distance form the earth

    d. None of the above

29. Terrestrial planets are

    a. Made of rock

    b. Have people on them

    c. The earth and no others

    d. The same size as Earth

30. How many planets orbit the sun in less than 224.7 days?

   a. 1 planet
   b. Only Venus
   c. 2 planets
   d. 3 planets

Strategy 9 - Try Every Option

For definition questions, try out all the options - one option will fit better than the rest. As you go through the options, use Strategy 5 - Elimination, to eliminate obviously incorrect choices as you go

Directions: Read the passage below, and answer the questions using this strategy.

Some of the common weather patterns on Earth are rain, wind, fog, and snow. Other weather patterns, generally classified as natural disasters, are hurricanes, tornadoes, typhoons and ice storms. Weather generally happens in the lower portion of the atmosphere, called the troposphere. Some weather occurs in the upper atmosphere, or stratosphere, where it can effect weather in the lower troposphere.

The principle cause of weather is different temperature, barometric pressure and moisture densities in the atmosphere. Weather phenomena in the atmosphere such as the jet stream, is caused by temperature differences in the tropical and polar air, which causes air to move from one to the other. The jet stream generally flows in a Western direction, and there are two or three jet streams in the Northern and Southern Hemispheres at any time.

Instabilities in the flow of the jet stream cause weather systems such as extra-tropical cyclones. Different processes cause weather systems such as monsoons or thunderstorms. Differences in temperature over land and over sea cause monsoons.

Due to the tilt of the Earth's axis, sunlight reaches the Earth at different angles at different times of the year, creating seasons. In January, the Northern Hemisphere is tilted away from the sun, so sunlight is more direct than in July.

31. The troposphere is

    a. The highest strata of the atmosphere

    b. The lowest strata of the atmosphere

    c. The middle level of the atmosphere

    d. Not part of the atmosphere

32. Monsoons are

    a. Caused by instabilities in the jet stream

    b. Caused by processes other than instabilities in the jet stream

    c. Part of the jet stream

    d. Cause the jet stream

33. Extra-tropical cyclones occur

    a. In the tropics

    b. In temperate zones

    c. In the gulf stream

    d. In mid-latitudes

34. Tilted means:

    a. Slanted

    b. Rotating

    c. Connected to

    d. Bent

Strategy 10 - Work for it

For questions about supporting details, work is the key. Review the passage to locate the right option. Never forget the choices that you are given are designed to confuse, and they may *seem* reasonable answers. However, if they are not mentioned in the text, they are "red herring" answers.

The best answer is the exact answer mentioned in the text.

Directions: Read the passage below, and answer the questions using this strategy.

Ebola is a common term for a group of viruses in the genus Ebola (EBOV), family Filoviridae. There are several species within the Ebola virus genus, with specific strains. Ebola is also a general term for the disease the viruses cause, Ebola hemorrhagic fever. The Ebola virus is transmitted through bodily fluids.

The Ebola virus interferes with the cell and patients die of hypovolemic shock.

The Ebola viruses are similar to the Marburg virus, also in the family Filoviridae. Most viruses are spherical, however, the Ebola viruses have long filaments. The Ebola and Marburg viruses have similar symptoms.

The first outbreak of Ebola occurred near the Ebola River, in the Democratic Republic of the Congo, which the disease and viruses are named after. Ebola is a very serious illness, very contagious and often fatal. The 2014 West African Ebola viral epidemic was the most widespread in history.

The Zaire virus was the first discovered in 1976 and is the most lethal. Ebola first emerged in 1976 in Zaire. An outbreak in Reston, Virginia brought the virus to international attention.

35. The Ebola virus received this name because of

    a. The doctor who first discovered the virus

    b. The cure that is used to treat those infected

    c. The river where the disease was first encountered

    d. What the virus does to the body

36. Viruses in the Ebola genus are recognizable

    a. Because of their hooked shape

    b. Because of their long filaments

    c. Due to their oblong heads

    d. Because of their unique color

37. One of the most common causes of death from the Ebola family of viruses is

    a. Hypovolemic shock due to blood vessel damage

    b. Bleeding of the brain that cannot be stopped

    c. A heart attack from blood loss and lack of fluids

    d. A high fever that cannot be lowered

38. The deadliest strain of the Ebola virus family is the

    a. The Reston strain

    b. The Ivory Coast strain

    c. The Zaire strain

    d. The Sudan strain

Strategy 11 - Look at the Big Picture

Details can be tricky when dealing with main idea and summary questions, but do not let the details distract you. Look at the big picture instead of the smaller parts to determine the right answer.

Directions: Read the passage below, and answer the questions using this strategy.

In 2005 researchers found three species of fruit bat carrying the Ebola virus, but not showing disease symptoms. These three species are called natural host, or reservoir species. Scientists have studied plants, insects and birds as potential reservoir species without success. Bats are the only reservoir species scientists have found. Apparently, bats are reservoir species for several viruses.

The first outbreaks, in 1976 and 1979, were in cotton factories where bats lived. Bats were also present in the Marburg infections in 1975 and 1980.

39. The species most suspected as a potential Ebola virus reservoir is

    a. Birds

    b. Insects

    c. Plants

    d. Bats

40. Most plant and animal species

    a. Can carry the Ebola virus but not become infected

    b. Can not carry and transmit the Ebola virus

    c. Are responsible for new cases of Ebola viruses

    d. Can be infected with one of the Ebola viruses

41. Bats are known for

    a. Being carriers of many different viruses, including Ebola

    b. Transmitting the Ebola virus through a scratch

    c. Being susceptible to the virus and becoming infected

    d. Transmitting the Ebola virus through infected droppings

Strategy 12 - Best Possible Answer

Determine the best answer according to the information given in the passage. Do not be distracted by answers that seem correct or are mostly correct.

Directions: Read the passage below, and answer the questions using this strategy.

Ebola may not be contagious initially but as the disease progresses, bodily fluids are extremely contagious.

Lack of proper equipment and proper hygiene has caused epidemics in poor and isolated areas. Unfortunately, infectious reservoirs generally exist in areas do not have modern hospitals or educated medical staff, adding to the chance of epidemics.

42. Ebola is highly contagious

    a. Only when blood is present

    b. Only in the first stages before hemorrhaging occurs

    c. At all stages of the illness from incubation to recovery

    d. Only in the later stages

43. Exposure to the Ebola virus means

    a. A death sentence for most patients

    b. Isolation for the patient, and proper precautions for all medical personnel to contain the virus

    c. The virus will spread rapidly and there is no treatment available

    d. A full recovery usually, with very few symptoms

44. Ebola outbreaks commonly occur

a. Because sterilization and containment procedures are not followed or available

b. Due to infected animals in the area

c. Because of rat droppings in homes

d. Because of a contaminated water supply

45. Ebola is

a. a. More common in advanced nations where treatment makes the disease minor

b. b. More common in third world and developing countries

c. c. Fatal in more than ninety-five percent of the cases

d. d. Highly contagious during the incubation period

Answers to Multiple-Choice Strategy Questions

Strategy 1 - Keywords in the question tell what the question is asking

1. B
The question asks about the free range *method* of farming. Here method refers to *type* of farming. "Method" here is the keyword and can be marked or underlined.

2. D
The Question is, "Free-range farming is *practiced* ..." The keyword here is "practiced." Looking at the choices, which all start with "to," it is clear the answer will be about *why* free range ... Also notice that one choice is "All of the above," which here, is the correct answer. However, when "All of the above" is an option, this is a potential Elimination Strategy. All you have to do is find one choice that is incorrect and you can use Strategy 5 - Elimination to eliminate two choices and increase your odds from one in four, to one in two.

3. A
The question is, "Free range farming husbandry ..." From the question, and the *lack* of keywords, together with the choices presented, the answer will be a definition free range farming husbandry.

4. C
The question is, "Free-range certification is *most important* to farmers because ... " The keywords here are "most important." Circle the keywords to keep them clear in your mind. Be careful to choose the best answer.

Strategy 2 - Watch Negatives

These four questions all have negatives: does not mean, is never, do not, and is not. These questions exclude possibilities, so if you see any choices that are true, you can eliminate them right away.

5. D

The question asks what sexual dimorphism does *not* mean. Circle the word "not" and keep it firmly in mind. Next, what is sexual dimorphism. Reading the text quickly, sexual dimorphism is related to the female bears being smaller than the males. Probably there are other aspects, but this general definition is all that is needed to answer the question.

First, notice that "All of the above" is choice D. In addition, the question is a negative. So, for choice D to be correct, choices A, B and C must be *in*correct. This narrows the choices. If any of choices A, B or C are correct, then you can eliminate that choice as well as choice D.

Either all the choices are *in*correct, in which case, choice D, "All of the above" is correct.

Choice A, male and females are the same size is incorrect. Choice B, all grizzly bears look the same and are the same size, is incorrect. Choice C, grizzly bears (plural so *all* grizzly bears) can be large and weigh more than half a ton. This is incorrect, since, while all grizzly bears are large, female bears weight less than half a ton.

All three choices are incorrect so choice D is the correct answer, "All of the Above," are incorrect.

6. A

First, circle or underline never to show this is a negative question. Now look at the options to find an option that is not true.

Choice A is true as male bears are 1,000 pounds. Place a mark beside this one. It may be tempting to select this option as your answer, but it is important to look at all choices before making a final decision.

Choice B is not true - size does not depend on the sex.
Choice C is not true - size does not depend on diet.
Choice D is not true - males often stand 8 feet.

So choice A is correct.

7. A
First circle "do not" to mark this as a negative question.

Choice A is correct, Yukon River grizzly bears do not get as big as other grizzlies, so put a mark beside it for later consideration. Examine the other choices before making a final decision.

Choice B is not mentioned in the text, and can be eliminated.

Choice C is not mentioned in the text and can be eliminated.

Choice D is true, but this is a negative question so it is false.

Some of the above choices may be true from a common sense point of view, but if they aren't mentioned specifically in the passage, they can be eliminated.

Choice A is correct.

Strategy 3 - Read the Stem Completely

Read the question, and then look for the answer in the text before reading the choices. Reading the choices first will confuse, just as it is meant to do! Do not fall into this trap!

8. B
The choices here are very confusing and are meant to be! Four variations on the Latin species name, Ursus Arctos are given, so the question is what version of this Latin name is correct, which gives a very straight-forward strategy to solving. Since the name is Latin, it is going to stand out in the text. Take the first option, "Arctas Ursinas," and scan the text for something that looks like that. At the end of the second sentence is "Ursus Arctos," which is very close. Next confirm what this sentence refers to, which gives the correct answer, choice B.

9. D
This question asks why Kodiak brown bears are a different subspecies, and the options are designed to confuse a careless, stressed test-taker. Scan the text for "Kodiak," which

appears in the second-to-last sentence, and answers the question.

10. C
This question asks about the relationship between brown bears and grizzly bears. If you are not careful you will be confused by the choices.

11. A
Read the question, then read the text before trying to answer and avoid confusion.

Strategy 4 - Consider all Choices Before Deciding

In Strategy 3, we learned to find the correct answer in the text before reading the choices. Now you have read the text and have the right answer. The next thing is Strategy 4 - Read *all* the choices. Once you have read all the choices, select the correct choice.

12. D
First, notice that "All of the above" is a choice. So if you find one option that is incorrect, you can eliminate that option and option D, "All of the above." Reading the question first, (Strategy #3) then looking in the text, and then reading all the choices before answering, you can see that choices A, B and C are all correct, so choice D, All of the Above, is the correct choice.
If you had not read all the choices first, then you might be tempted to impulsively choose A, B, or C.

13. C
Looking at the choices, they are designed to confuse with different choices and combinations. Recognizing this, it is therefore important to be extra careful in making your choice. If you are stressed, in a hurry, or not paying attention, you will probably get this question wrong by making an impulsive choice and not reading through all the choices before making a selection.

Referring to the text, you will find the sentence, "... it was a hybrid, with the mother a polar bear and the father a grizzly," which answers the question.

14. D

Reading through all the choices, B and C can be eliminated right away as they are not mentioned in the text. They might appear as good answers but they are not from the passage.

Looking at choices A and D, the issue is if this has happened before, or has it happened only in zoos. Referring to the text, the second paragraph tells us it is the first hybrid found in the wild.

15. B

Reading through the four choices, the question concerns, what does science know? Does it happen all the time? Completely understood? They do survive? Is it possible? Look in the text for how much is known. The last sentence, "Until 2006, there had been no documented cases of a grizzly polar bear hybrid found in the wild." gives the answer.

Strategy 5 - Elimination

For every question, no matter what type, eliminating obviously incorrect answers narrows the possible choices. Elimination is probably the most powerful strategy for answering multiple-choice.

16. A

Using this strategy the choices can be narrowed down to choices A and D. I have never seen a peacock with red in their tail, so choice C can *probably* be eliminated, but check back. Most birds and many animals have a pattern where the male is colorful and the female less colorful. Choice B can be eliminated as it refers to "both sexes" having colorful tails. Choice D is a good candidate as the text refers to molting season, however, the text does not say how long this is, so there is some doubt. This makes choice A the best choice as it is referred to directly in the text.

17. B

Choice D can be eliminated right away, as a male bird to sit on eggs is not mentioned in the text.

Skimming the passage, choices A and C can be eliminated,

as they are not mentioned directly in the text, leaving only choice D.

18. C
Choices A, B and D can be eliminated right away, as the passage states the peacock is the male bird. Referring to the text, "plumage and train of the male peafowl, or peacock ..." making choice C the best choice.

19. D
Choices A and B can be eliminated either right away or with a quick check of the passage, since they are not mentioned. Choice C is suspicious since the grey feathers are under the tail feathers, so it is difficult to see how they could be visible when the tail feathers are lowered.

Strategy 6 - Opposites

If there are opposites, one of them is generally the correct answer. If it helps, make a table that lays out the different options and the correct option will become clear.

20. D
Notice that choices A and D are opposites. Referring to the text, "Smallpox is a highly infectious disease unique to humans ..." eliminates choice A. Also notice choices B and C are not mentioned in the text and can be eliminated right away.

21. C
Notice that all the choices are opposites. 30% - 35% mortality, or survival rate, or 60%. Therefore, the task is to review the text, looking for 30% or 60%, survival or mortality, stay clear, and do not get confused. Sometimes making notes or a table can help to clarify.

The question is asking about percent, so it is easy and fast to skim the passage for a percent sign.

The first percent sign is in the fourth paragraph, 30% - 35%. Write this in the margin. Next, see what this percent refers to, which is the mortality rate. Write "mortality" next to 30% - 35%. Now, working backwards, see what the 30% - 35%

mortality rate refers to. At the beginning of that sentence, is Variola Major.

| 30% - 35% | Mortality | V. Major |

Now we have a clear understanding of what the passage is saying, which we have retrieved quickly and easily, and hopefully will not be confused by the different choices.

Choices A and B can be eliminated right away. Choice C looks correct. Check choice D quickly, and confirm that it is incorrect. Choice C is the correct answer.

22. B
Choices A and B are opposites. Is Variola Minor more or less severe, with more or fewer pox, and more or less scarring? The other two choices, "no pox" and "no treatment" can be eliminated quickly. Either choice A or B are going to be wrong.

Make a quick table like this:

Major - more serious - scars, blindness
Minor - milder

The passage does not mention scarring from Variola minor, but we can infer that it is milder. Looking at the options, choice A is clearly talking about Variola major, and we can infer that choice B is talking about Variola minor and is the correct answer. We can confirm our inference from the text.

Also note the words, 'major' and 'minor.' Which gives a clue concerning severity, and the elimination of choice A.

23. A
Choices A and B are not exactly opposite, but very close and designed to confuse if you do not read them properly. How many people die from the virus? Between 30% and 35%? Or between 35% and 60%? Scan the text with these numbers in mind.

This question is asking about a percent, so quickly scan the passage for a percent sign, which first appears in the second paragraph. Working back, confirm that the percent figures that you quickly found is related to mortality, which it is.

Strategy 7 - Look for Differences

Look at two choices that appear to be correct and examine them carefully.

24. B
Choices A, B and C are very similar and designed to confuse and distract someone who does not look carefully at the text. What is astraphobia exactly? This is a definition question for an unusual word, astraphobia. Scan the text for "astraphobia." Choice B is correct.

25. C
Choices A, B and C are similar and designed to confuse, or tempt a stressed or careless test-taker into making a quick and incorrect choice. Checking the passage, in the first paragraph, lightning occurs in thunderstorms, volcanic eruptions and in dust storms, so choice C is correct.

26. C
All four answers are similar and designed to confuse. Seeing how similar the choices are, it is very important to be clear on the exact definition. Scan the text quickly for the word "fulgurites." From the third paragraph, "This is hot enough to turn sand, some soils or even rock into hollow glass channels..." so the correct answer, and the option that answers the question best, is choice C.

Strategy 8 - Context Clues

Look at the sentences and the context to determine the best option. Sometimes, the answer may be located right in the passage or question.

27. B
You do not have to know the exact meaning - just enough to answer the question. The phrase is used in the passage, "Venus, as the second brightest star in the sky, after the moon, reaches an apparent magnitude of −4.6 ..." where Venus is compared to the brightness of the moon, so the apparent magnitude must have something to do with brightness,

which is enough information to answer the question. Notice also, how the choices are opposites. Choice A and B are opposites as are choices C and D.

28. A
The exact meaning is not necessary, you only need only enough information to answer the question. The passage where this phrase is used is, "Venus is an inferior planet from Earth, meaning that it is closer to the sun: its elongation reaches a maximum of 47.8°." Elongation in this sentence is something connected with distance from the sun, but also something to do with Earth. Choice C can be eliminated right away, and since one choice is wrong, Choice D, All of the Above, can also be eliminated. Choice A is the best answer since it mentions, "as seen from earth."

29. A
Choices C and D can be eliminated right away. No mention is made of size or people, so choices C and D are also incorrect. Terrestrial has many similar meanings, but choice A is the best. From the passage, "Venus is one of the four solar terrestrial planets, or rocky bodies that orbit the sun."

Note that choice B is a grammatical error and can be eliminated right away. The question is, "Terrestrial planets are," and choice B is, "Have people on them."

This is a great strategy, looking for grammatical errors and eliminating, and what you might expect to see on a test that a professor has made themselves. However, most standardized tests are generated by computer, and proofed by many different people who have considerable expertise in correcting this type of easy question. Keep this in mind because it is an easy elimination, but don't expect to see this type of thing on a standardized test.

30. A
This is a bit of a trick question and designed to confuse, as it requires an additional step of logical reasoning. Referring to the text, Venus is the *second* closest planet to the sun so there must be one planet that is closer. Planets closer to the sun will rotate the sun faster, so the answer must be choice A.

Strategy 9 - Try Every Option for Word Meaning Questions

For definition questions, try out all the options - one option will fit better than the rest. As you go through the options, use Strategy 5 - Elimination, to eliminate obviously incorrect choices as you go.

31. B
The answer is taken directly from the passage. Notice that choices A and B are opposites, so one of them will be incorrect. Look in the text carefully for the exact definition. If you are uncertain, make a table in the margin.

Scan the passage looking for the word you are asked to define. Large or unusual words generally stand out and can be located quickly. Once you have found the position in the passage of the word using quick reading or scanning techniques, then focus on the sentence and read carefully.

32. B
The sentences talking about the jet stream and monsoons are next to one another. Trying each definition, and comparing to the text, only choice B fits. If you are uncertain, copy the information from the passage into a table.

The question is, what is the relationship between monsoons and the jet stream.

Scan the passage for "jet stream" and "monsoon."

Tropical cyclones	Jet stream
Monsoons and thunderstorms	Different processes

33. D
Referring to the passage, and trying each definition choice, choice D is the only answer that makes sense referring to the text.

34. A
The passage from the text is, "Due to the tilt of the Earth's axis, sunlight reaches the Earth at different angles at dif-

ferent times of the year, creating seasons." Substituting all the choices given into this sentence, slanted, choice A, is the only sensible answer. Here is what substitutions look like:

> a. In June the Northern Hemisphere is *slanted* towards the sun...
>
> b. In June the Northern Hemisphere is *rotating* towards the sun...
>
> c. In June the Northern Hemisphere is *connected to* towards the sun...
>
> d. In June the Northern Hemisphere is *bent* towards the sun...

Choice A is the only one that makes sense.

Strategy 10 - You Have to Work for it! Check Carefully for Supporting Details

All answers can be found by carefully reading the text. The questions paraphrase the text found in the passage.

35. C
The passage has a lot of details so read carefully and stay clear.

36. B
The choices are designed to confuse. Check the text for the exact definition and do not be distracted by other choices.

37. A
Here is a quick tip. On choice A, the word hypovolemic is used. This is an unusual word and specific medical vocabulary. None of the other choices uses any specific vocabulary like this, so it is very likely to be the right answer. You can quickly scan the text for this word to confirm. Scanning the text for an unusual word is easy and fast, and one of the most powerful techniques for this type of question.

38. C
Scan the text for Zaire.

Strategy 11 - Look at the Big Picture

Details can be tricky when dealing with main idea and summary questions, but do not let the details distract you. Look at the big picture instead of the smaller parts to determine the right answer.

39. D
The passage says in 2005 it was found there are 3 fruit bat species most suspected of carrying the virus. The details (3 species, fruit bats and 2005) do not matter. Only the fact that bats are suspected.

40. B
The relevant passage is, "Scientists have studied plants, insects and birds as potential reservoir species without success. Bats are the only reservoir species scientists have found." The inference is that these plant and animal species cannot be infected, (i.e. carry and transmit the disease) so choice B is correct.

41. A
The relevant passage is,Apparently, bats are reservoir species for several viruses.

Strategy 12 - Make the Best Choice Based on the Information Given

42. D
Choices B and C are incorrect by the passage, "In the early stages, Ebola may not be highly contagious."Choice A is not mentioned, leaving choice D.

43. B
Choices A and D are obviously incorrect and can be eliminated right away. Choice C is irrelevant to the question.

44. A
Choices B and C are not mentioned in the passage. Choice D is a good possibility, however, choice A covers choice D and is mentioned in the text.

45. B
Choice A is incorrect. Choices C and D are not mentioned.

Basic Math Multiple-Choice Strategy

Math is the one section where you need to make sure that you understand the processes before you ever tackle it. That's because the time allowed on the math portion is typically so short that there's not much room for error. It's imperative that before the test day arrives, you've learned all the main formulas that will be used, and then created your own problems that utilize the formula and then solved them.

On the actual test day, use the "Plug-Check-Check" strategy. Here's how it goes.

Read the problem, but not the answers. You'll want to work the problem first and come up with your own answers. If you did the work right, you should find your answer among the options given.

If you need help with the problem, plug actual numbers into the variables given. You'll find it easier to work with numbers than it is to work with letters. For instance, if the question asks, "If Y - 4 is 2 more than Z, then Y + 5 is how much more than Z?" try selecting a value for Y. Let's take 6. Your question now becomes, "If 6 - 4 is 2 more than Z, then 6 plus 5 is how much more than Z?" Now your answer should be easier to work with.

Check the answer options to see if your answer matches one of those. If so, select it.

If no answer matches the one you got, re-check your math, but this time, use a different method. In math, it's common for there to be more than one way to solve a problem. As a simple example, if you multiplied 12 X 13, and did not get an answer that matches one choice, you might try adding 13 together 12 different times and see if you get a good answer.

Math Multiple-Choice Strategy

The two strategies for working with basic math multiple-choice are Estimation and Elimination.

Math Strategy 1 - Estimation

Just like it sounds, try to estimate an approximate answer first. Then look at the choices.

Math Strategy 2 - Elimination

For every question, no matter what type, eliminating obviously incorrect answers narrows the possible choices. Elimination is probably the most powerful strategy for answering multiple-choice.

Here are a few basic math examples of how this works.

Solve 2/3 + 5/12

    a. 9/17
    b. 3/11
    c. 7/12
    d. 1 1/12

First Estimate. 2/3 is more than half and 5/12 is about half, so the answer is going to be very close to 1.

Next, Eliminate. Choice A is about 1/2 and can be eliminated, Choice B is very small, less than 1/2 and can be eliminated. Choice C is close to 1/2 and can be eliminated. Leaving only choice D, which is just over 1.

Work through the solution, a common denominator is needed, a number which both 3 and 12 will divide into.
2/3 = 8/12. So, 8 + 5/12 = 13/12 = 1 1/12
Choice D is correct.

Here is another example:

Solve 4/5 – 2/3

    a. 2/2
    b. 2/13
    c. 1
    d. 2/15

You can eliminate choice A, because it is 1 and since both of the numbers are close to one, the difference is going to be very small. You can eliminate choice C for the same reason.

Next, look at the denominators. Since 5 and 3 don't go into 13, you can eliminate Choice B as well.

That leaves choice D.

Checking the answer, the common denominator will be 15. So (12 - 10)/15 = 2/15. Choice D is correct.

Fractions shortcut - Cancelling Out

In any operation with fractions, if the numerator of one fractions has a common multiple with the denominator of the other, you can cancel out. This saves time and simplifies the problem quickly, making it easier to manage.

Solve 2/15 ÷ 4/5

    a. 6/65
    b. 6/75
    c. 5/12
    d. 1/6

To divide fractions, we multiply the first fraction with the inverse of the second fraction. Therefore we have 2/15 x 5/4. The numerator of the first fraction, 2, shares a multiple with the denominator of the second fraction, 4, which is 2. These cancel out, which gives, 1/3 x 1/2 = 1/6

Cancelling Out solved the questions very quickly, but we can still use multiple-choice strategies to answer.

Choice B can be eliminated because 75 is too large a denominator. Choice C can be eliminated because 5 and 15 don't go in to 12.

Choice D is correct.

Decimal Multiple-Choice strategy and Shortcuts.

Multiplying decimals gives a very quick way to estimate and eliminate choices. Anytime that you multiply decimals, it is going to give an answer with the same number of decimal places as the combined operands.

So for example,

2.38 X 1.2 will produce a number with three places of decimal, which is 2.856.
Here are a few examples with step-by-step explanation:

Solve 2.06 x 1.2

    a. 24.82
    b. 2.482
    c. 24.72
    d. 2.472

This is a simple question, but even before you start calculating, you can eliminate several choices. When multiplying decimals, there will always be as many numbers behind the decimal place in the answer as the sum of the ones in the initial problem, so choices A and C can be eliminated.

The correct answer is D: 2.06 x 1.2 = 2.472

Solve 20.0 ÷ 2.5

    a. 12.05
    b. 9.25
    c. 8.3
    d. 8

First estimate the answer to be around 10, and eliminate choice A. And since it'd also be an even number, you can eliminate choices B and C, leaving only choice D.

The correct Answer is D: 20.0 ÷ 2.5 = 8

Answer Sheet

	A	B	C	D	E			A	B	C	D	E
1	○	○	○	○	○		21	○	○	○	○	○
2	○	○	○	○	○		22	○	○	○	○	○
3	○	○	○	○	○		23	○	○	○	○	○
4	○	○	○	○	○		24	○	○	○	○	○
5	○	○	○	○	○		25	○	○	○	○	○
6	○	○	○	○	○							
7	○	○	○	○	○							
8	○	○	○	○	○							
9	○	○	○	○	○							
10	○	○	○	○	○							
11	○	○	○	○	○							
12	○	○	○	○	○							
13	○	○	○	○	○							
14	○	○	○	○	○							
15	○	○	○	○	○							
16	○	○	○	○	○							
17	○	○	○	○	○							
18	○	○	○	○	○							
19	○	○	○	○	○							
20	○	○	○	○	○							

Basic Math Strategy Practice Questions

1. Solve 1/4 + 11/16

    a. 9/16
    b. 1 1/16
    c. 11/16
    d. 15/16

2. Solve 7/11 + 3/11

    a. 6/11
    b. 9/11
    c. 10/11
    d. 4/11

3. Solve 5/9 + 2/9

    a. 6/11
    b. 1 3/7
    c. 7/18
    d. 7/9

4. Solve 3/12 + 11/12

    a. 6/12
    b. 1/6
    c. 1 1/6
    d. 1 3/12

5. Solve 13/16 − 1/4

    a. 1
    b. 12/12
    c. 9/16
    d. 7/16

6. Solve 17/23 − 15/23

    a. 2
    b. 1/11
    c. 2/13
    d. 2/23

7. Solve 13/15 − 7/15

    a. 3/5
    b. 7/15
    c. 2/5
    d. 6

8. 33/49 − 23/49

    a. 10/49
    b. 11/49
    c. 10
    d. 13/23

9. Solve 3/4 X 5/11

    a. 2/15
    b. 10/44
    c. 3/19
    d. 15/44

10. Solve 6/10 x 5/16

    a. 4/15
    b. 3/16
    c. 2 1/3
    d. 2/7

11. Solve 3/7 x 4/7

    a. 6/27
    b. 12/49
    c. 3/19
    d. 2/7

12. Solve 4/5 x 2/5

    a. 5/21
    b. 6/25
    c. 8/25
    d. 1 3/5

13. Solve 5/8 ÷ 2/3

    a. 15/16
    b. 10/24
    c. 5/12
    d. 1 2/5

14. Solve 11/20 ÷ 9/20

    a. 99/20
    b. 4 19/20
    c. 1 2/9
    d. 1 1/9

15. Solve 7.25 x 0.5

    a. 3.625
    b. 3.526
    c. 36.25
    d. 35.25

16. Solve 21.02 x 0.34

    a. 71.468
    b. 7.1468
    c. 7.48
    d. 714.68

17. Solve 3.4 ÷ 1.7

    a. 12.05
    b. 9.25
    c. 8.3
    d. 2

18. Solve 2.4 + 3.9

    a. 6.3
    b. 7.3
    c. 5.3
    d. 6.13

19. Solve 3.34 + 2.13

    a. 54.7
    b. 5.57
    c. 5.47
    d. 54.7

Basic Math Multiple Choice

20. Solve 42.87 − 26.401

    a. 9.033
    b. 90.33
    c. 73.03
    d. 69.271

21. Solve 6.363 - 1.602

    a. 4.011
    b. 4.761
    c. 47.61
    d. 3.761

22. Solve 67.54 − 43.45

    a. 24.09
    b. 24.19
    c. 24.019
    d. 23.09

23. Convert 75% to decimal

    a. 0.0075
    b. 0.075
    c. 0.75
    d. 7.5

24. Convert 39% to decimal

    a. 0.309
    b. 0.039
    c. 3.9
    d. 0.39

25. What is 25% of 135?

    a. 33.75
    b. 25
    c. 60
    d. 45.35

Answer Key

1. D
Since 9 is less than 11, you can eliminate choice A because an addition problem means that the final number won't be less than the initial numbers in the problem. And since 11 is equal to 11, you can eliminate choice C, based on that the sum would be a higher number than the ones you started out with.

Narrowing it down between choice B and D. From the two numbers, you can see that something over a whole number is going to be too high, which just leaves choice D.

Do the calculations to confirm.
A common denominator is needed, a number which both 4 and 16 will divide into. So, 4 + 11/16 = 15/16

2. C
Since 4, 6, and 9 are all less than the sum of 7 + 3, you can eliminate choice A, B, and D.

Do the calculations to confirm.
Since the denominators are the same, we can just add the numerators, so 7 + 3/11 = 10/11

3. D
You can eliminate choices A and B right away, since 9 does not go in to 11 or 7, so even if you needed to find a common denominator, neither one of those would be what you were looking for.

9 does go into 18, but it would mean you'd have to multiply everything by 2, and that would be equal to more than 7 when you added the numerators together.

Do the calculations to confirm. Since the denominators are the same, we can just add the numerators, so 5 + 2/9 = 7/9

4. C
Choice A can be eliminated because 11/12 by itself is more than one half. Choice B can be eliminated because it is so

close to 0, that 11/12 almost being a whole number means it cannot be 1/6.

Do the calculations to confirm.
Since the denominators are the same, we can just add the numerators, so 3 + 11/12 = 14/12 = 1 2/12 = 1 1/6

5. C
Choices A and B can both be eliminated because that are 1 and the difference of two fractions is not going to be 1.

Do the calculations to confirm.
A common denominator' is needed, number which both 16 and 4 will divide into. So 1(3 - 4)/16 = 9/16

6. D
Choice A can be eliminated because 2 is a whole number, which would not be the difference between two subtracted fractions. Choices B and C can be eliminated since, neither 11 or 13 go into 23.

Do the calculations to confirm.
Since the denominators are the same, subtract the numerators, so (17 - 15)/23 = 2/23

7. C
You can eliminate choice D because it is a whole number. Since choice B is the same as one of the fractions in the problem, you can eliminate that, since subtracting it is not going to equal a number in the problem.

Do the calculations to confirm.
Since the denominators are the same, subtract the numerators, so (13 - 7)/15 = 6/15 = 2/5

8. A
Choice C can be eliminated as it is a whole number. Choice D can be eliminated because 23 does not go evenly in to 49.

Do the calculations to confirm.
Since the denominators are the same, subtract the numerators, so (33 - 23)/49 = 10/49

9. D
Since 15 and 19 are not common denominators with 4 or 11, choices A and C can be eliminated.

Do the calculations to confirm.
Since there are no common numerators and denominators to cancel out, multiply the numerators and then the denominators. So 3 x 5/4 x 11 = 15/44

10. B
Choice C can be eliminated because multiplying fractions does not give whole numbers. 15 and 7 are not common denominators with 10 or 16, so choices A and D can be eliminated as well.

Do the calculations to confirm.
Since there are common numerators and denominators to cancel out, 6/10 x 5/16 to get 6/2 x 1/16 = 3/2 x 1/8, and multiply numerators and denominators to get 3/16

11. B
Choice D can be eliminated because 2 is less than the product of 3 and 4. Since 7 doesn't go in to 27 or 19, choices A and C can be eliminated.

Do the calculations to confirm.
Since there are no common numerators and denominators to cancel out, we simply multiply the numerators and then the denominators. So 3 x 4/7 x 7 = 12/49

12. C
Since there are no common numerators and denominators to cancel out, we simply multiply the numerators and then the denominators. So 4 x 2/5 x 5 = 8/25

Since multiplying fractions won't produce whole numbers, choice D can be eliminated. Since 5 does not divide evenly into 21, choice A can be eliminated.

13. A
Choice D can be eliminated because it is a number greater than 1. Dividing fractions is just flipping one and multiplying by the other, so choice C can be eliminated since 5 as

the numerator is too small. Since you have to flip the second fraction, choice B can be eliminated as well, as that's just multiplying straight across.

Do the calculations to confirm.
To divide fractions, we multiply the first fraction with the inverse of the second fraction. Therefore 5/8 x 3/2 = 15/16

14. C
Choice A can be eliminated because 99 is the produce of 11 and 9, which would not be multiplied in this problem. Choice B can be eliminated because 4 is too high of a number.

Do the calculations to confirm.
11/20 x 20/9 = 11/1 x 1/9 = 11/9 = 1 2/9

15. A
When multiplying decimals, there should be as many numbers behind the decimal place in the answer, as the sum of the ones in the initial problem, choices C and D can be eliminated. Since it's a multiple of 5, the last number would be 5 and not 6, eliminating choice B.

Do the calculations to confirm.
7.25 x 0.5 = 3.625

16. B
When multiplying decimals, there should be as many numbers behind the decimal place in the answer, as the sum of the ones in the initial problem, choices A C, and D can be eliminated.

Do the calculations to confirm.
21.02 x 0.34 = 7.1468

17. D
Since the estimate of this would be around 1.5, choices A, B, and C are all too high to be the answer.

Do the calculations to confirm.
3.4 ÷ 1.7 = 2

18. A
A quick estimate of equation would be about 6. Choice B is too high and can be eliminated. Choice C is too low, and can be eliminated.

Do the calculations to confirm.
2.4 + 3.9 = 6.3

19. C
A quick estimate would be about 5, which would make choices A and D too high to be the answer.

Do the calculations to confirm.
3.34 + 2.13 = 5.47

20. D
Choice A is too small to be the sum of the two larger numbers and can be eliminated. The estimate of this problem would be about 70, so choices B and C would be too high of a sum.

Do the calculations to confirm.
42.87 + 26.401 = 69.271

21. B
Choice C can be eliminated as it is larger than the starting numbers. 1.602 is about half of 3, so you can eliminate choice D for being too small of a number.

Do the calculations to confirm.
6.363 - 1.602 = 4.761

22. A
Choice C can be eliminated because there are too many numbers after the decimal place.

Do the calculations to confirm.
67.54 − 43.45 = 24.09

23. C
Since 75% can also be written as 75/100, choice D can be eliminated because 75/100 cannot be a whole number. Choices A and B are too small of numbers to be 75/100.

Do the calculations to confirm.

To convert percent to decimal, simply divide the decimal by 100 or move the decimal point 2 places to the left. Therefore, 75 ÷ 100 = 0.75

24. D
Since you can write 39% as 39/100, choice C can be eliminated because a part of 100 will not be a whole number. Choice B is too small of a number to be 39/100.

Do the calculations to confirm.
To convert percent to decimal, simply divide the decimal by 100 or move the decimal point 2 places to the left. Therefore, 39 ÷ 100 = 0.39

25. A
Choice C is close to about 50% of 135, so it can be eliminated. Choice B is 25% of 100, so it can be eliminated as well. Choice D is close to 50 and would be about 33% of 135, leaving you with choice A.

Do the calculations to confirm.
25/100 x 135 = 25 x 1.35 = 33.75

Fraction Tips, Tricks and Shortcuts

When you remember that fractions are just numbers, they aren't so intimidating. Here are some ideas to keep in mind as you work through fraction math problems:

Remember that a fraction is just a number which names a portion of something. For instance, instead of having a whole pie, a fraction says you have a part of a pie--such as a half of one or a fourth of one.

Two digits make up a fraction. The digit on top is known as the numerator. The digit on the bottom is known as the denominator. To remember which is which, just remember that "denominator" and "down" both start with a "d." And the "downstairs" number is the denominator. So for instance, in ½, the numerator is the 1 and the denominator (or "downstairs") number is the 2.

- It's easy to add two fractions if they have the same denominator. Just add the digits on top and leave the bottom one the same: 1/10 + 6/10 = 7/10.

- It's the same with subtracting fractions with the same denominator: 7/10 - 6/10 = 1/10.

- Adding and subtracting fractions with different denominators is more complicated. First, you have to get the problem so that they do have the same denominators. The easiest way to do this is to multiply the denominators: For 2/5 + 1/2 multiply 5 by 2. Now you have a denominator of 10. But now you have to change the top numbers too. Since you multiplied the 5 in 2/5 by 2, you also multiply the 2 by 2, to get 4. So the first number is now 4/10. Since you multiplied the second number times 5, you also multiply its top number by 5, to get a final fraction of 5/10. Now you can add 5 and 4 together to get a final sum of 9/10.

- Sometimes you'll be asked to reduce a fraction to its simplest form. This means getting it to where the only common factor of the numerator and denominator is 1. Think of it this way: Numerators and denominators are brothers that must be treated the same. If you do something to one, you must do it to the other, or it's just not fair. For instance, if you divide your numerator by 2, then you should also divide the denominator by the same. Let's take an example: The fraction 2/10 . This is not reduced to its simplest terms because there is a number that will divide evenly into both: the number 2. We want to make it so that the only number that will divide evenly into both is 1. What can we divide into 2 to get 1? The number 2, of course! Now to be "fair," we have to do the same thing to the denominator: Divide 2 into 10 and you get 5. So our new, reduced fraction is 1/5.

- In some ways, multiplying fractions is the easiest of all: Just multiply the two top numbers and then multiply the two bottom numbers. For instance, with this problem: 2/5 X 2/3 you multiply 2 by 2 and get a top number of 4; then multiply 5 by 3 and get a bottom number of 15. Your answer is 4/15.

- Dividing fractions is more involved, but still not too hard. You once again multiply, but only AFTER you have turned the second fraction upside-down. To divide ⅞ by ½, turn the ½ into 2/1, then multiply the top numbers and multiply the bottom numbers: ⅞ X 2/1 gives us 14 on top and 8 on the bottom.

Converting Fractions to Decimals

There are a couple of ways to become good at converting fractions to decimals. One -- the one that will make you the fastest in basic math skills -- is to learn some basic fraction facts. It's a good idea, if you're good at memory, to memorize the following:

1/100 is "one hundredth," expressed as a decimal, it's .01.

1/50 is "two hundredths," expressed as a decimal, it's .02.

1/25 is "one twenty-fifths" or "four hundredths," expressed as a decimal, it's .04.

1/20 is "one twentieth" or ""five hundredths," expressed as a decimal, it's .05.

1/10 is "one tenth," expressed as a decimal, it's .1.

1/8 is "one eighth," or "one hundred twenty-five thousandths," expressed as a decimal, it's .125.

1/5 is "one fifth," or "two tenths," expressed as a decimal, it's .2.

1/4 is "one fourth" or "twenty-five hundredths," expressed as a decimal, it's .25.

1/3 is "one third" or "thirty-three hundredths," expressed as a decimal, it's .33.

1/2 is "one half" or "five tenths," expressed as a decimal, it's .5.

3/4 is "three fourths," or "seventy-five hundredths," expressed as a decimal, it's .75.

Of course, if you're no good at memorization, another good technique for converting a fraction to a decimal is to manipulate it so that the fraction's denominator is 10, 10, 1000, or some other power of 10. Here's an example: We'll start with ¾. What is the first number in the 4 "times table" that you can multiply and get a multiple of 10? Can you multiply 4 by something to get 10? No. Can you multiply it by something to get 100? Yes! 4 X 25 is 100. So let's take that 25 and multiply it by the numerator in our fraction ¾. The numerator is 3, and 3 X 25 is 75. We'll move the decimal in 75 all the way to the left, and we find that ¾ is .75.

We'll do another one: 1/5. Again, we want to find a power of 10 that 5 goes into evenly. Will 5 go into 10? Yes! It goes 2 times. So we'll take that 2 and multiply it by our numerator, 1, and we get 2. We move the decimal in 2 all the way to the left and find that 1/5 is equal to .2.

Converting Fractions to Percent

Working with fractions or percent can be intimidating enough. But converting from one to the other? That's a genuine nightmare for those who are not math wizards. But really, it doesn't have to be that way. Here are two ways to make it easier to convert a fraction to a percent.

- First, you might remember that a fraction is nothing more than a division problem: you're dividing the bottom number into the top number. So for instance, if we start with a fraction 1/10, we are making a division problem with the 10 on the outside the bracket and the 1 on the inside. As you remember from your lessons on dividing by decimals, since 10 won't go into 1, you add a decimal and make it 10 into 1.0. 10 into 10 goes 1 time, and since it's behind the decimal, it's .1. And how do we say .1? We say "one tenth," which is exactly what we started with: 1/10. So we have a number we can work with now: .1. When we're dealing with percents, though, we're dealing strictly with hundredths (not tenths). You remember from studying decimals that adding a zero to the right, on the right side of the decimal does not change the value. Therefore, we can change .1 into .10 and have the same number--except now it's expressed as hundredths. We have 10 hundredths. That's ten out of 100--which is just another way of saying ten percent (ten per hundred or ten out of 100). In other words .1 = .10 = 10 percent. Remember, if you're changing from a decimal to a percent, get rid of the decimal on the left and replace it with a percent mark on the right: 10%. Let's review those steps again: Divide 10 into 1. Since 10 doesn't go into 1, turn 1 into 1.0. Now divide 10 into 1.0. Since 10 goes into 10 1 time, put it there and add your decimal to make it .1. Since a percent is always "hundredths," let's change .1 into .10. Then remove the decimal on the left and replace with a percent sign on the right. The answer is 10%.

- If you are doing these conversions on a multiple-choice test, here's an idea that might be even easier and faster. Let's say you have a fraction of 1/8 and you're asked what the percent is. Since we know that "percent" means hundredths, ask yourself what number we can multiply 8 by to get 100. Since there is no number, ask what number gets us close to 100. That number is 12: 8 X 12 = 96. So it gets us a little less than 100. Now, whatever you do to the denominator, you have to do to the numerator. Let's multiply 1 X 12 and we get 12. However, since 96 is a little less than 100, we know that our answer will be a percent a little MORE than 12%. So if your possible answers on the multiple-choice test are these:

a) 8.5%   b) 19%   c) 12.5%   d) 25%

then we know the answer is c) 12.5%, because it's a little MORE than the 12 we got in our math problem above.

Another way to look at this, using multiple-choice strategy is you know the answer will be "about" 12. Looking at the other choices, they are all too large or too small and can be eliminated right away.

This was an easy example to demonstrate, so don't be fooled! You probably won't get such an easy question on your exam, but the principle holds just the same. By estimating your answer quickly, you can eliminate choices immediately and save precious exam time.

Decimal Tips, Tricks and Shortcuts

Converting Decimals to Fractions
One of the most important tricks for correctly converting a decimal to a fraction doesn't involve math at all. It's simply to learn to say the decimal correctly. If you say "point one" or "point 25" for .1 and .25, you'll have more trouble getting the conversion correct. If it's called "one tenth" and "twenty-five hundredths," you're on the way to a correct conversion. That's because, if you know your fractions, you know that "one tenth" looks like this: 1/10. And "twenty-five hundredths" looks like this: 25/100.

Even if you have digits before the decimal, such as 3.4,

learning how to say the word will help you with the conversion into a fraction. It's not "three point four," it's "three and four tenths." Knowing this, you know that the fraction which looks like "three and four tenths" is 3 4/10.

Of course, your conversion is not complete until you reduce the fraction to its lowest terms: It's not 25/100, but 1/4.

Converting Decimals to Percent

Changing a decimal to a percent is easy if you remember one math formula: multiply by 100. For instance, if you start with .45, you change it to a percent by simply multiplying it by 100. You then wind up with 45. Add the % sign to the end and you get 45%.

That seems easy enough, right? Here think of it this way: You just take out the decimal and stick in a percent sign on the opposite sign. In other words, the decimal on the left is replaced by the % on the right.

It doesn't work quite that easily if the decimal is in the middle of the number. Let's use 3.7 for example. Here, take out the decimal in the middle and replace it with a 0 % at the end. So 3.7 converted to decimal is 370%.

Percent Tips, Tricks and Shortcuts

Percent problems are not nearly as scary as they appear, if you remember this neat trick:

Draw a cross as in:

Portion	Percent
Whole	100

In the upper left, write PORTION. In the bottom left, write WHOLE. In the top right, write PERCENT and in the bottom right, write 100. Whatever your problem is, you will leave blank the unknown, and fill in the other four parts. For example, let's suppose your problem is: Find 10% of 50. Since we know the 10% part, we put 10 in the percent corner. Since the whole number in our problem is 50, we put that in the corner marked whole. You always put 100 underneath the percent, so we leave it as is, which leaves only the top left corner blank. This is where we'll put our answer. Now simply multiply the two corner numbers that are NOT 100. Here, it's 10 X 50. That gives us 500. Now divide this by the remaining corner, or 100, to get a final answer of 5. 5 is the number that goes in the upper-left corner, and is your final solution.

Another hint to remember: Percents are the same thing as hundredths in decimals. So .45 is the same as 45 hundredths or 45 percent.

Converting Percents to Decimals

Percents are simply a specific type of decimals, so it should be no surprise that converting between the two is actually fairly simple. Here are a few tricks and shortcuts to keep in mind:

- Remember that percent means "per 100" or "for every 100." So when you speak of 30% you are saying 30 for every 100 or the fraction 30/100. In basic math, you learned that fractions that have 10 or 100 as the denominator can easily be turned into a decimal. 30/100 is thirty hundredths, or expressed as a decimal, .30.
- Another way to look at it: To convert a percent to a decimal, simply divide the number by 100. So for instance, if the percent is 47%, divide 47 by 100. The result will be .47. Get rid of the % mark and you're done.
- Remember that the easiest way of dividing by 100 is by moving your decimal two spots to the left.

Converting Percents to Fractions

Converting percents to fractions is easy. After all, a percent is a type of fraction; it tells you what part of 100 that you're talking about. Here are some simple ideas for making the conversion from a percent to a fraction:

- If the percent is a whole number -- say 34% -- then simply write a fraction with 100 as the denominator (the bottom number). Then put the percentage itself on top. So 34% becomes 34/100.
- Now reduce as you would reduce any percent. Here, by dividing 2 into 34 and 2 into 100, you get 17/50.
- If your percent is not a whole number -- say 3.4% --then convert it to a decimal expressed as hundredths. 3.4 is the same as 3.40 (or 3 and forty hundredths). Now ask yourself how you would express "three and forty hundredths" as a fraction. It would, of course, be 3 40/100. Reduce this and it becomes 3 2/5.

Word Problem Multiple-Choice Strategy

Most students find word problems difficult. Solving word problems is much easier if you have a systematic approach which we outline below.

Here is the biggest tip for studying Word problems.

Practice regularly and systematically. Sounds simple and easy right? Yes it is, and yes it really does work.

Word problems are a way of thinking and require you to translate a real word problem into mathematical terms.

Some math instructors go so far as to say that learning how to think mathematically is the main reason for teaching word problems.

So what do we mean by Practice regularly and systematically? Studying word problems and math in general requires a logical and mathematical frame of mind. The only way that you can get this is by practicing regularly, which means everyday.

It is critical that you practice word problems everyday for the 5 days before the exam as a bare minimum.

If you practice and miss a day, you have lost the mathematical frame of mind and the benefit of your previous practice is pretty much gone. Anyone who has studied math will agree – you have to practice everyday.

Everything is important. The other critical point about word problems is that all the information given in the problem has some purpose. There is no unnecessary information! Word problems are typically around 50 words in 1 to 3 sentences. If the sometimes complicated relationships are to be explained in that short an explanation, every word has to count. Make sure that you use every piece of information.

Here are 9 simple steps to solve word problems.

Step 1 – Read through the problem at least three times. The first reading should be a quick scan, and the next two readings should be done slowly to find answers to these important questions:

What does the problem ask? (Usually located towards the end of the problem)

What does the problem imply? (This is usually a point you were asked to remember).

Mark all information, and underline all important words or phrases.

Step 2 – Try to make a pictorial representation of the problem such as a circle and an arrow to show travel. This makes the problem a bit more real and sensible to you.

A favorite word problem is something like, 1 train leaves Station A travelling at 100 km/hr. and another train leaves Station B travelling at 60 km/hr. ...

Draw a line, the two stations, and the two trains at either end. This will help clarify the situation in your mind.

Step 3 – Use the information you have to make a table with a blank portion to show information you do not know.

Step 4 – Assign a single letter to represent each unknown data in your table. You can write down the unknown that each letter represents so that you do not make the error of assigning answers to the wrong unknown, because a word problem may have multiple unknowns and you will need to create equations for each unknown.

Step 5 – Translate the English terms in the word problem into a mathematical algebraic equation. Remember that the main problem with word problems is that they are not expressed in regular math equations. You ability to identify correctly the variables and translate the word problem into an equation determines your ability to solve the problem.

Step 6 – Check the equation to see if it looks like regular equations that you have seen before, and whether it looks sensible. Does the equation appear to represent the information in the question? Take note that you may need to rewrite some formulas needed to solve the word problem equation. For example, word distance problems may need rewriting the distance formula, which is Distance = Time x Rate. If the word problem requires that you solve for time you will need to use Distance/Rate and Distance/Time to solve for Rate. If you understand the distance word problem you should be able to identify the variable you need to solve for.

Step 7 – Use algebra rules to solve the derived equation. Take note that the laws of equation demands that what is done on this side of the equation has to also be done on the other side. You have to solve the equation so that the unknown ends up alone on one side. Where there are multiple unknowns you will need to use elimination or substitution methods to resolve all the equations.

Step 8 – Check your final answers to see if they make sense with the information given in the problem. For example if the word problem involves a discount, the final price should be less or if a product was taxed then the final answer has to cost more.

Step 9 – Cross check your answers by placing the answer or answers in the first equation to replace the unknown or unknowns. If your answer is correct then both side of the equation must equate or equal. If your answer is not correct then you may have derived a wrong equation or solved the equation wrongly. Repeat the necessary steps to correct.

Types of Word problems

Word problems can be classified into 12 types. Below are examples of each type with a complete solution. Some types of Word problems can be solved quickly using multiple-choice strategies and some cannot. Always look for ways to estimate the answer and then eliminate choices.

1. Age

A girl is 10 years older than her brother. By next year, she will be twice the age of her brother. What are their ages now?

    a. 25, 15
    b. 19, 9
    c. 21, 11
    d. 29, 19

Solution: B

We will assume that the girl's age is "a" and her brother's is "b." This means that based on the information in the first sentence,
$a = 10$

Next year, she will be twice her brother's age, which gives
$a + 1 = 2(b + 1)$

We need to solve for one unknown factor and then use the answer to solve for the other. To do this we substitute the value of "a" from the first equation into the second equation. This gives

$10 + b + 1 = 2b + 2$
$11 + b = 2b + 2$
$11 - 2 = 2b - b$
$b = 9$

$9 = b$ this means that her brother is 9 years old. Solving for the girl's age in the first equation gives

$a = 10 + 9$
$a = 19$ the girl is aged 19. So, the girl is aged 19 and the boy is 9

2. Distance or speed

Two boats travel down a river towards the same destination, starting at the same time. One boat is traveling at 52 km/hr, and the other boat at 43 km/hr. How far apart will they be after 40 minutes?

    a. 46.67 km
    b. 19.23 km
    c. 6.03 km
    d. 14.39 km

Solution: C

After 40 minutes, the first boat will have traveled = 52 km/hr. x 40 minutes/60 minutes = 34.7 km

After 40 minutes, the second boat will have traveled = 43 km/hr. x 40/60 minutes = 28.66 km

Difference between the two boats will be 34.7 km – 28.66 km = 6.03 km

Multiple-Choice Strategy

First estimate the answer. The first boat is travelling 9 km. faster than the second, for 40 minutes, which is 2/3 of an hour. 2/3 of 9 = 6, as a rough guess of the distance apart.

Choices A, B and D can be eliminated right away.

3. Ratio

The instructions in a cookbook states that 700 grams of flour must be mixed in 100 ml of water, and 0.90 grams of salt added. A cook however has just 325 grams of flour. What is the quantity of water and salt that he should use?

    a. 0.41 grams and 46.4 ml
    b. 0.45 grams and 49.3 ml
    c. 0.39 grams and 39.8 ml
    d. 0.25 grams and 40.1 ml

Solution: A

The Cookbook states 700 grams of flour, but the cook only has 325. The first step is to determine the percentage of flour he has 325/700 x 100 = 46.4%
That means that 46.4% of all other items must also be used.
46.4% of 100 = 46.4 ml of water
46.4% of 0.90 = 0.41 grams of salt.

Multiple-Choice Strategy

The recipe calls for 700 grams of flour but the cook only has 325, which is just less than half, so the quantity of water and salt are going to be about half.

Choices C and D can be eliminated right away. Choice B is very close so be careful. Looking closely at Choice B, it is exactly half, and since 325 is slightly less than half of 700, it can't be correct.

Choice A is correct.

4. Percent

An agent received $6,685 as his commission for selling a property. If his commission was 13% of the selling price, how much was the property?

    a. $68,825
    b. $121,850
    c. $49,025
    d. $51,423

Solution: D

Let's assume that the property price is x
That means from the information given, 13% of x = 6,685
Solve for x,
x = 6685 x 100/13 = $51,423

Multiple-Choice Strategy

The commission, 13%, is just over 10%, which is easier to work with. Round up $6685 to $6700, and multiple by 10 for an approximate answer. 10 X 6700 = $67,000. You can

do this in your head. Choice B is much too big and can be eliminated. Choice C is too small and can be eliminated. Choices A and D are left and good possibilities.
Do the calculations to make the final choice.

5. Sales & Profit

A store owner buys merchandise for $21,045. He transports them for $3,905 and pays his staff $1,450 to stock the merchandise on his shelves. If he does not incur further costs, how much does he need to sell the items to make $5,000 profit?

   a. $32,500
   b. $29,350
   c. $32,400
   d. $31,400

Solution: D

Total cost of the items is $21,045 + $3,905 + $1,450 = $26,400
Total cost is now $26,400 + $5000 profit = $31,400

Multiple-Choice Strategy

Round off and add the numbers up in your head quickly. 21,000 + 4,000 + 1500 = 26500. Add in 5000 profit for a total of 31500.

Choice B is too small and can be eliminated. Choice C and Choice A are too large and can be eliminated.

6. Tax/Income

A woman earns $42,000 per month and pays 5% tax on her monthly income. If the Government increases her monthly taxes by $1,500, what is her income after tax?

   a. $38,400
   b. $36,050
   c. $40,500
   d. $39,500

Solution: A

Initial tax on income was 5/100 x 42,000 = $2,100
$1,500 was added to the tax to give $2,100 + 1,500 = $3,600
Income after tax left is $42,000 - $3,600 = $38,400

7. Interest

A man invests $3000 in a 2-year term deposit that pays 3% interest per year. How much will he have at the end of the 2-year term?

    a. $5,200
    b. $3,020
    c. $3,182.7
    d. $3,000

Solution: C

This is a compound interest problem. The funds are invested for 2 years and interest is paid yearly, so in the second year, he will earn interest on the interest paid in the first year.

3% interest in the first year = 3/100 x 3,000 = $90
At end of first year, total amount = 3,000 + 90 = $3,090
Second year = 3/100 x 3,090 = 92.7.
At end of second year, total amount = $3090 + $92.7 = $3,182.7

8. Averaging

The average weight of 10 books is 54 grams. 2 more books were added and the average weight became 55.4. If one of the 2 new books added weighed 62.8 g, what is the weight of the other?

    a. 44.7 g
    b. 67.4 g
    c. 62 g
    d. 52 g

Solution: C

Total weight of 10 books with average 54 grams will be=10×54=540 g
Total weight of 12 books with average 55.4 will be=55.4×12=664.8 g
So the total weight of the remaining 2 will be= 664.8 – 540 = 124.8 g
If one weighs 62.8, the weight of the other will be= 124.8 g – 62.8 g = 62 g

Multiple-Choice Strategy

Averaging problems can be estimated by looking at which direction the average goes. If additional items are added and the average goes up, the new items much be greater than the average. If the average goes down after new items are added, the new items must be less than the average.

Here, the average is 54 grams and 2 books are added which increases the average to 55.4, so the new books must weight more than 54 grams.

Choices A and D can be eliminated right away.

9. Probability

A bag contains 15 marbles of various colors. If there are 3 white marbles, 5 red, and the rest are black, what is the probability of randomly picking out a black marble from the bag?

    a. 7/15
    b. 3/15
    c. 1/5
    d. 4/15

Solution: A

Total marbles = 15
Number of black marbles = 15 – (3 + 5) = 7
Probability of picking out a black marble = 7/15

10. Two Variables

A company paid a total of $2850 to book 6 single and 4 double rooms for one night. Another company paid $3185 to book for 13 single rooms for one night in the same hotel. What is the cost for single and double rooms in that hotel?

    a. single= $250 and double = $345
    b. single= $254 and double = $350
    c. single = $245 and double = $305
    d. single = $245 and double = $345

Solution: D

We can determine the price of single rooms from the information given of the second company. 13 single rooms = 3185.
One single room = 3185 / 13 = 245
The first company paid for 6 single rooms at $245. 245 x 6 = $1470
Total amount paid for 4 double rooms by first company = $2850 - $1470 = $1380
Cost per double room = 1380 / 4 = $345

11. Geometry

The length of a rectangle is 5 in. more than its width. The perimeter of the rectangle is 26 in. What is the width and length of the rectangle?

    a. width = 6 inches, Length = 9 inches
    b. width = 4 inches, Length = 9 inches
    c. width =4 inches, Length = 5 inches
    d. width = 6 inches, Length = 11 inches

Solution: B

Formula for perimeter of a rectangle is 2(L + W)
p=26, so 2(L + W) = p
The length is 5 inches more than the width, so
2(w + 5) + 2w = 26
2w + 10 + 2w = 26
2w + 2w = 26 - 10

$4w = 16$

$W = 16/4 = 4$ inches

L is 5 inches more than w, so $L = 5 + 4 = 9$ inches.

12. Totals and fractions

A basket contains 125 oranges, mangos and apples. If 3/5 of the fruits in the basket are mangos and only 2/5 of the mangos are ripe, how many ripe mangos are there in the basket?

    a. 30
    b. 68
    c. 55
    d. 47

Solution: A
Number of mangos in the basket is 3/5 x 125 = 75
Number of ripe mangos = 2/5 x 75 = 30

Answer Sheet

	A	B	C	D
1	○	○	○	○
2	○	○	○	○
3	○	○	○	○
4	○	○	○	○
5	○	○	○	○
6	○	○	○	○
7	○	○	○	○
8	○	○	○	○
9	○	○	○	○
10	○	○	○	○

Practice Questions

1. The average weight of 13 students in a class of 15 (two were absent that day) is 42 kg. When the remaining two are weighed, the average became 42.7 kg. If one of the remaining students weighs 48 kg., how much does the other weigh?

    a. 44.7 kg.
    b. 45.6 kg.
    c. 46.5 kg.
    d. 41.4 kg.

2. Brad has agreed to buy everyone a Coke. Each drink costs $1.89, and there are 5 friends. Estimate Brad's cost.

    a. $7
    b. $8
    c. $10
    d. $12

3. At the beginning of 2009, Madalyn invested $5,000 in a savings account. The account pays 4% interest per year. How much will Madalyn have in the account in 2 years?

    a. $5,408
    b. $5,200
    c. $5,110
    d. $7,000

4. The cost of waterproofing canvas is .50 a square yard. What's the total cost for waterproofing a canvas truck cover that is 15' x 24'?

   a. $18.00
   b. $6.67
   c. $180.00
   d. $20.00

5. John is a barber and receives 40% of the amount paid by each of his customers, and all tips. If a customer pays $8.50 for a haircut and tips $1.30, how much money does John receive?

   a. $3.92
   b. $4.70
   c. $5.70
   d. $6.40

6. Two trains start their journey at the same time, one with average speed of 72 km/hr. and other with 52 km/hr. How far apart are the trains after 20 minutes?

   a. 6.67 km
   b. 17.33 km
   c. 24.3 km
   d. 41.33 km

7. John purchased a jacket at a 7% discount. He had a membership and received an additional discount of 1.6%. If he paid $425, what is the retail price of the jacket?

   a. $448
   b. $460
   c. $466
   d. $472

8. A store sells stereos for $545. If 15% of the cost was added to the price as value-added tax, what is the total cost?

   a. $490.4
   b. $626.75
   c. $575.00
   d. $590.15

9. A car covers a certain distance in 3.5 hours at an average speed of 60 km/hr. How much time in hours will a motorbike take to cover the same distance at an average speed of 40 km/hr.?

   a. 4.5
   b. 4.75
   c. 5.25
   d. 5

10. Jim left home for the office at 7:00 am. He reached his office at 7:48 am. How far is his house from office if his average driving speed is 40 km./hr.?

   a. 32 km
   b. 34 km
   c. 38 km
   d. 40 km

Answer Key

1. C
Total weight of 13 students with average 42 will be = 42 × 13 = 546 kg.
Total weight of 15 students with average 42.7 will be = 42.7 × 15 = 640.5 kg. So the total weight of the remaining 2 will be = 640.5 - 546 = 94.5 kg. Weight of the other will be = 94.5 − 48 = 46.5 kg

Multiple-Choice Strategy

When the 2 additional students were added, the average went up, so they must weigh more than the average. Choice D is less than the average so it can be eliminated right away.

2. C
If there are 5 friends and each drink costs $1.89, we can round up to $2 per drink and estimate the total cost at, 5 X $2 = $10.

The actual, cost is 5 X $1.89 = $9.45.

3. A
This is a compound interest problem. Interest is paid out at the end of the first year and added to the account, and then interest is paid on the new total in the second year.

First do a quick calculation in your head, using numbers that are easy to work with. 5000 X 10% = 500 and so 5% will be half of that which is $250. If we ignore the compounding (interest on interest) in the second year, we have an approximate total of $5500, which is a high approximation.

Choice D can be eliminated as much too high, and choice C is too low. Choice B is about the total for one years interest so it can also be eliminated. Choice A is the only choice left.

Do the calculations to confirm.

5000 X 4% = 200

In the second year, 5200 X 4% = 208
So the total at the end of the second year is $5,408.

4. D
This is a square foot cost problem. The problem is to find the total square footage, and the multiply by the cost.

Use math shortcuts to calculate the answer in your head. First calculate total square feet, which is 15 * 24 = 360 ft². Next, convert this value to square yards, (1 yards² = 9 ft²) which is 360/9 = 40 yards². At $0.50 per square yard, the total cost is 40 * 0.50 (or half) = $20.

5. B
Estimate the answer in your head quickly. 40% is close to 50%, which is half. 50% of $8.50 is 4.25 plus tips of $1.30 is 5.55 approximately.

Looking at the options, choices A and D can all be eliminated as too low or too high, leaving choice B and C. C is probably too high, as 5.55 is an approximation and so choice B is looking correct.

Do the calculations to confirm.
8.5 X 40/100 = 3.40 + 1.30 = $4.70.

6. A
First estimate the answer quickly in your head. One train is travelling at 72 km. and the other at 52 km. In one hour they will be 20 km. apart, so in 20 minutes they will be 20/3 = about 6.5 km.

Looking at the options, choices B and C are far to big and can be eliminated. Choice D is closer, but still too large, and can also be eliminated.

Do the calculations to confirm.
Distance traveled by 1st train in 20 minute
= (72 km/hr. × 20 minutes)/60 minutes = 24 km.
Distance traveled by 2nd train in 20 minute
= (52 km./hr. × 20 minutes)/60 minutes = 17.33 km.
Difference in distance = 24 - 17.33 = 6.67 km.

7. C
Make a rough estimate in your head. Use 10% instead of 7%, so 425 + 10% = 467. Ignore the 1.6% for now and remember this is an estimate on the high side.

Choice A is too small and can be eliminated and choice D is too high and can be eliminated. That leaves choices B and C.

Do the calculations to confirm.
Let the original price be x, then at rate of 7% the discounted price will be = 0.93x
2% discounted amount then will be = 0.02 × 0.93x = 0.0186x
Remaining price = 0.93x - 0.0186x = 0.9114x
This is the amount which John has paid so
0.9114x = 425
x = 425/ 0.9114
x = $466.31

8. B
This question can be estimated in your head with a few shortcuts. 15% is difficult to work with so use 10% and 5%.
10% of 545 = 54.5
5% of 545 = about 27 (half of 10%)
Add them quickly in your head by estimating again. Take 50 + 25 = 75 and add 7 for a rough approximation of 82. The actual number is 81.5.
Add 82 to 545. Again round to easy numbers to work with. take 550 + 82 = 632. Remember this is a high estimate. (The actual figure is 626.5)

Looking at the options, the only choice over 600 is Choice B.

Confirm by doing the calculations.
Actual cost = X, therefore, X = 545 + (545 X 0.15)
X = 545 + 81.75
X = 626.75

9. C
Estimate the answer first. The car is travelling at 60 km. and the motorbike is travelling at 40 km., which is 2/3 (40/60 = 2/3, or 2:3). So the motorcycle will take one-third

longer to travel the same distance. If the car took 3.5 hours, the motorbike will take 3.5 + (1/3 of 3.5). 1/3 of 3.5 is going to be about 1.1, or say 1. 3.5 + 1 = 4.5.

Looking at the options, choice D can be eliminated right away. Choice A can be eliminated since it equals our estimate.

Do the calculations to confirm.
The distance covered by the car = 60 X 3.5 = 210 km.
Time required by the motorbike = 210/40 = 5.25 hr.

10. A
Do a quick estimate in your head and see if any options can be eliminated. Jim is travelling for 48 minutes at 40 km. per hour. If he was travelling for one hour, he would cover 40 km. Right away choice D can be eliminated because he is only travelling for a portion of an hour. Choice C, 38 km. is a very unlikely choice because it is so close to 40 and can be eliminated. The answer will be choice A or B.

Do the calculations to confirm.
Time to reach the office = 48 minutes. So if he covers 40 km in 60 minutes, then in 48 minutes, he will cover 48 X 40/60 = 32 km.

How to Improve your Vocabulary

VOCABULARY TESTS CAN BE DAUNTING WHEN YOU THINK OF THE ENORMOUS NUMBER OF WORDS THAT MIGHT COME UP IN THE EXAM. As the exam date draws near, your anxiety will grow because you know that no matter how many words you memorize, chances are, you will still remember so few, and there are so many more to memorize! Here are some tips which you can use to hurdle the big words that may come up in your exam without having to open the dictionary and memorize all the words known to humankind.

Build up and tear apart the big words. Big words, like many other things, are composed of small parts. Some words are made up of many other words. A man who lifts weights for example, is a weight lifter. Words are also made up of word parts, called prefixes, suffixes and roots. Often times, we can see the relationship of different words through these parts. A person who is skilled with both hands is ambidextrous. A word with double meaning is ambiguous. A person with two conflicting emotions is valent. Two words with synonymous meanings often have the same root. Bio, a root word derived from Latin, is used in words like biography meaning to write about a person's life, and biology meaning the study of living organisms.

- **Words with double meanings.** Did you know that the word husband not only means a man married to a woman, but also thrift or frugality? Sometimes, words have double meanings. The dictionary meaning, or the denotation of a word is sometimes different from the way we use it or its connotation.

- **Read widely, read deeply and read daily.** The best way to expand your vocabulary is to familiarize yourself with as many words as possible through reading. By reading, you are able to remember words in a proper context and thus, remember its meaning or at the very least, its use. Reading widely would help you get acquainted with words you may never use every day. This is the best strategy without doubt. However, if you are studying for an exam next week, or even tomorrow, it isn't much help! Below you will find a range of different ways to learn new words quickly and efficiently.

- **Remember.** Big words are easy to understand when divided into smaller parts, and the smaller words will often have several other meanings aside from the one you already know. Below is an extensive list of root or stem words, followed by practice questions.

Here are suggested effective ways to help you improve your vocabulary.

Be Committed To Learning New Words. To improve your vocabulary you need to make a commitment to learn new words. Commit to learning at least a word or two a day. You can also get new words by reading books, poems, stories, plays and magazines. Expose yourself to more language to increase the number of new words that you learn.

- **Learn Practical Vocabulary**. As much as possible, learn vocabulary that is associated with what you do and that you can use regularly. For example, learn words related to your profession or hobby. Learn as much vocabulary as you can in your favorite subjects.

- **Use New Words Frequently**. When you learn a new word start using it and do so frequently. Repeat it when you are alone and try to use the word as often as you can with people you talk to. You can also use flashcards to practice new words that you learn.

- **Learn the Proper Usage.** If you do not understand the proper usage, look it up and make sure you have it right.

- **Use a Dictionary**. When reading textbooks, novels or assigned readings, keep the dictionary nearby. Also learn how to use online dictionaries and WORD dictionary. When you come across a new word, check for its meaning. If you cannot do so immediately, then you should right it down and check it as soon as possible. This will help you understand what the word means and exactly how best to use it.

- **Learn Word Roots, Prefixes and Suffixes.** English words are usually derived from suffixes, prefixes and roots, which come from Latin, French or Greek. Learning the root or origin of a word will help understand the meaning of the word and other words that are derived from the root. Generally, if you learn the meaning of one root word, you will understand two or three words. See our List of Stem Words below. This is a great two-for-one strategy. Most prefixes, suffixes, roots and stems are used in two, three or more words, so if you know the root, prefix or suffix, you can guess the meaning of many words.

- **Synonyms and Antonyms**. Most words in the English language have two or three (at least) synonyms and antonyms. For example, "big," in the most common usage, has about seventy-five synonyms and an equal number of antonyms. Understanding the relationships between these words and how they all fit together gives your brain a framework, which makes them easier to learn, remember and recall.

- **Use Flash Cards**. Flash cards are one of the best ways to memorize things. They can be used anywhere and anytime, so you can make use of odd free moments waiting for the bus or waiting in line. Make your own or buy commercially prepared flash cards, and keep them with you all the time.

- **Make word lists.** Learning vocabulary, like learning many things, requires repetition. Keep a new words journal in a separate section or separate notebook. Add any words that you look up in the dictionary, as well as from word lists. Review your word lists regularly.

Photocopying or printing off word lists from the Internet or handouts is not the same. Actually writing out the word and a few notes on the definition is an important process for imprinting the word in your brain. Writing out the word and definition in your New Word Journal, forces you to concentrate and focus on the new word. Hitting PRINT or pushing the button on the photocopier does not do the same thing.

Meaning in Context Answer Sheet

1. (A) B C D   21. A B C D
2. A B C D   22. A B C D
3. A B C D   23. A B C D
4. A B C D   24. A B C D
5. A B C D   25. A B C D
6. A B C D   26. A B C D
7. A B C D   27. A B C D
8. A B C D   28. A B C D
9. A B C D   29. A B C D
10. A B C D   30. A B C D
11. A B C D   31. A B C D
12. A B C D   32. A B C D
13. A B C D   33. A B C D
14. A B C D   34. A B C D
15. A B C D   35. A B C D
16. A B C D   36. A B C D
17. A B C D   37. A B C D
18. A B C D   38. A B C D
19. A B C D   39. A B C D
20. A B C D   40. A B C D

Meaning in Context

Meaning in context is a powerful tool for learning vocabulary. Essentially, you make an educated guess of the meaning from the context of the sentence. With meaning in context questions, also called sentence completion, you don't have to know the exact meaning - just an approximate meaning to answer the question.

This is also true is when reading. Sometimes it is necessary to know the exact meaning. Other times, the exact meaning is not important and you can make an educated guess from the context and continue reading.

The meaning in context exercises below give you practice making guesses about the meaning.

 Directions: For each of the questions below, choose the word with the meaning best suited to the sentence based on the context.

1. When Joe broke his _____ in a skiing accident, his entire leg was in a cast.

   a. Ankle
   b. Humerus
   c. Wrist
   d. Femur

2. Alan had to learn the _____ system of numbering when his family moved to Great Britain.

   a. American
   b. Decimal
   c. Metric
   d. Fingers and toes

3. After Lisa's aunt had her tenth child, Lisa found that she had more than twenty _____.

    a. Uncles

    b. Friends

    c. Stepsisters

    d. Cousins

4. Although he had flown many times, this was his first flight in a _____.

    a. Helicopter

    b. Kite

    c. Train

    d. Subway car

5. George is very serious about his _____, and recently joined the American Scholastic Association.

    a. Schoolwork

    b. Cooking

    c. Travelling

    d. Athletics

6. She was a rabid Red Sox fan, attending every game, and demonstrating her _____ by cheering more loudly than anyone else.

    a. Knowledge

    b. Boredom

    c. Commitment

    d. Enthusiasm

7. When Craig's dog was struck by a car, he rushed his pet to the _____.

    a. Emergency room

    b. Doctor

    c. Veterinarian

    d. Podiatrist

8. After she received her influenza vaccination, Nan thought that she was _____ to the common cold.

    a. Immune

    b. Susceptible

    c. Vulnerable

    d. At risk

9. Paul's rose bushes were being destroyed by Japanese beetles, so he invested in a good _____.

    a. Fungicide

    b. Fertilizer

    c. Sprinkler

    d. Pesticide

10. The last time that the crops failed, the entire nation experienced months of _____.

    a. Famine

    b. Harvest

    c. Plenitude

    d. Disease

11. Because of a pituitary dysfunction, Karl lacked the necessary _____ to grow as tall as his father.

    a. Glands

    b. Hormones

    c. Vitamins

    d. Testosterone

12. Because of its colorful fall _____ , the maple is my favorite tree.

    a. Growth

    b. Branches

    c. Greenery

    d. Foliage

13. When Mr. Davis returned from southern Asia, he told us about the _____ that   sometimes swept the area, bringing torrential rain.

    a. Monsoons

    b. Hurricanes

    c. Blizzards

    d. Floods

14. Is it true that _____ always grows on the north side of trees?

    a. Grass

    b. Moss

    c. Ferns

    d. Ground cover

15. You can _____ some fires by covering them with dirt, while others require foam or water.

    a. Extinguish

    b. Distinguish

    c. Ignite

    d. Lessen

16. Using powerful fans that circulate the heat over the food, _____ ovens work very efficiently.

    a. Microwave

    b. Broiler

    c. Convection

    d. Pressure

17. Because of the growing use of _____ as a fuel, corn production has greatly increased.

    a. Alcohol

    b. Ethanol

    c. Natural gas

    d. Oil

18. In heavily industrialized areas, the air pollution causes many _____ diseases.

    a. Respiratory

    b. Cardiac

    c. Alimentary

    d. Circulatory

19. Because hydroelectric power is a _____ source of energy, its use is considered a green energy.

    a. Significant

    b. Disposable

    c. Renewable

    d. Reusable

20. The process required the use of highly _____ liquids, so fire extinguishers were everywhere in the factory.

    a. Erratic

    b. Combustible

    c. Inflammable

    d. Neutral

21. I still don't know exactly. That isn't _____ evidence.

    a. Undeterred

    b. Unrelenting

    c. Unfortunate

    d. Conclusive

22. He could manipulate the coins in his fingers very _____.

    a. Brazenly

    b. Eloquently

    c. Boisterously

    d. Deftly

23. His investment scheme _____ many serious investors, who lost money.

    a. Helped

    b. Vindicated

    c. Duped

    d. Reproved

24. When we go to a party, we always _____ a driver.

    a. Feign

    b. Exploit

    c. Dote

    d. Designate

25. This new evidence should _____ any doubts.

    a. Dispel

    b. Dispense

    c. Evaluate

    d. Diverse

26. She went to Asia on $10 a day – her _____ travelling plans are amazing.

    a. Frothy

    b. Frugal

    c. Fraught

    d. Focal

27. My grandmother's house is full or trinkets and ornaments. She is always buying _____.

    a. Collectibles

    b. Baubles

    c. China

    d. Crystal

28. I am finally out of debt! I paid off all of my _____.

    a. Debtors

    b. Defendants

    c. Accounts Receivable

    d. Creditors

29. I love listening to his speeches. He has a gift for _____.

    a. Oratory

    b. Irony

    c. Jargon

    d. None of the above

30. The warehouse went bankrupt so all of the furniture has to be _____.

    a. Dissected

    b. Liquidated

    c. Destroyed

    d. Bought

31. He sold the property when he didn't even own it. The whole thing was a _____.

    a. Hoax

    b. Feign

    c. Defile

    d. Default

32. The repair really isn't working. Those parts you replaced are _____.

    a. Despondent

    b. Illusive

    c. Deficient

    d. Granular

33. Just because she is supervisor, doesn't mean we have to _____ in front of her.

    a. Foible

    b. Grovel

    c. Humiliate

    d. Indispose

34. That noise is _____ ! It is driving me crazy.

    a. Loud

    b. Intolerable

    c. Frivolous

    d. Fictitious

35. Her inheritance was a good size and included many _____.

    a. Heirlooms

    b. Perchance

    c. Cynical

    d. Lateral

36. I see that sign everywhere. It is much more _____ than I thought.

    a. Prelude
    b. Prevalent
    c. Ratify
    d. Rational

37. Her attitude was very casual and _____.

    a. Idle
    b. Nonchalant
    c. Portly
    d. Portend

38. The machine _____ the rock into ore.

    a. Quells
    b. Pulverizes
    c. Eradicates
    d. Segments

39. The water in the pond has been sitting for so long it is _____.

    a. Stagnant
    b. Sediment
    c. Stupor
    d. Residue

40. She didn't listen to a thing and _____ all the objections.

    a. Manipulated
    b. Mired
    c. Furtive
    d. Rebuffed

ANSWER KEY.

1. D
Femur NOUN A thighbone.

2. C
Metric System a system of measurements that is based on the base units of the meter/metre, the kilogram, the second, the ampere, the kelvin, the mole, and the candela.

3. D
Cousins NOUN the son or daughter of a person's uncle or aunt; a first cousin.

4. A
Helicopter

5. B
Schoolwork

6. D
Enthusiasm NOUN intensity of feeling; excited interest or eagerness.

7. C
Veterinarian NOUN medical doctor who treats non-human animals.

8. A
Immune ADJECTIVE protected by inoculation, or due to innate resistance to pathogens.

9. D
Pesticide NOUN a substance, usually synthetic although sometimes biological, used to kill or contain the activities of pests.

10. A
Famine NOUN a period of extreme shortage of food in a region.

11. B
Hormones NOUN any substance produced by one tissue and conveyed by the bloodstream to another to effect physiological activity.

12. D
Foliage NOUN the leaves of plants.

13. A
Monsoons NOUN tropical rainy season when the rain lasts for several months with few interruptions.

14. B
Moss NOUN any of various small green plants growing on the ground or on the surfaces of trees, stones etc.

15. A
Extinguish NOUN to put out, as in fire; to end burning; to quench.

16. C
Convection NOUN the vertical movement of heat and moisture.

17. B
Ethanol NOUN a type of alcohol used as fuel.

18. A
Respiratory NOUN relating to respiration; breathing.

19. D
Reusable NOUN able to be used again; especially after salvaging or special treatment or processing.

20. B
Combustible NOUN capable of burning.

21. D
Conclusive ADJECTIVE providing an end to something; decisive.

22. D
Deftly ADVERB quickly and neatly in action.

23. C
Dupe VERB to swindle, deceive, or trick.

24. D
Designate ADJECTIVE appointed; chosen.

25. A
Dispel VERB to drive away by scattering, or so to cause to vanish; to clear away.

26. B
Frugal ADJECTIVE cheap, economical, thrifty.

27. B
Baubles NOUN a cheap showy ornament.

28. D
Creditors NOUN a person to whom a debt is owed.

29. A
Oratory NOUN the art of public speaking, especially in a formal, expressive, or forceful manner.

30. B
Liquidate VERB to convert assets into cash.

31. A
Hoax NOUN to deceive (someone) by making them believe something which has been maliciously or mischievously fabricated.

32. C
Deficient ADJECTIVE lacking something essential.

33. B
Grovel VERB to abase oneself before another person.

34. B
Intolerable ADJECTIVE not capable of being borne or endured; not proper or right to be allowed; insufferable; insupportable; unbearable.

35. A
Heirloom NOUN A valued possession that has been passed down through the generations.

36. B
Prevalent ADJECTIVE Widespread.

37. B
Nonchalant ADJECTIVE Casually calm and relaxed.

38. B
Pulverizes VERB to completely destroy, especially by crushing to fragments or a powder.

39. A
Stagnant ADJECTIVE lacking freshness, motion, flow, progress, or change; stale; motionless; still.

40. D
Rebuff NOUN a sudden resistance or refusal. [12]

Word List 1 – The Top 100 Common Vocabulary

Learning vocabulary, especially in a hurry for an exam, means that you will be making friends with a lot of different word lists. Below is a word list of top 100 "must know" vocabulary to get you started.

When studying word lists, think of different ways to mix-it-up. Work with a friend or a study group and compare word lists and test each other, or make flash cards.

1. **Abate** VERB reduce or lesson.
2. **Abandon** VERB to give up completely.
3. **Aberration** NOUN something unusual, different from the norm.
4. **Abet** VERB to encourage or support.
5. **Abstain** VERB to refrain from doing something.
6. **Abrogate** VERB to abolish or render void.
7. **Aesthetic** ADJECTIVE pertaining to beauty.
8. **Abstemious** ADJECTIVE moderate in the use of food or drink.
9. **Anachronistic** ADJECTIVE out of the context of time, out of date.
10. **Acrimonious** ADJECTIVE sharp or harsh in language or temper.
11. **Asylum** NOUN sanctuary, place of safety.
12. **Banal** ADJECTIVE lacking in freshness, originality, or vigor.
13. **Bias** NOUN a prejudice towards something or against something.
14. **Belie** VERB to give a false idea of.
15. **Brazen** ADJECTIVE bold.
16. **Belligerent** ADJECTIVE engaged in war.
17. **Camaraderie** NOUN togetherness, trust, group dynamic of trust.
18. **Cabal** NOUN a small group of persons engaged in plotting.
19. **Capacious** ADJECTIVE very large, spacious.
20. **Callous** ADJECTIVE unfeeling or insensitive.

21. **Clairvoyant** ADJECTIVE can predict the future.
22. **Cantankerous** ADJECTIVE ill-natured; quarrelsome.
23. **Compassion** NOUN sympathy.
24. **Captious** ADJECTIVE quick to find fault about trifle.
25. **Condescending** ADJECTIVE patronizing.
26. **Chauvinist** NOUN an extreme patriot.
27. **Conformist** NOUN someone who follows the majority.
28. **Clamorous** VERB loud and noisy.
29. **Deleterious** ADJECTIVE harmful.
30. **Deference** NOUN submitting to the wishes or judgment of another.
31. **Digression** NOUN straying from main point.
32. **Delectable** ADJECTIVE very pleasing.
33. **Discredit** NOUN dishonor someone, prove something untrue.
34. **Demeanor** NOUN behavior; bearing.
35. **Divergent** ADJECTIVE moving apart, going in different directions.
36. **Edict** NOUN a public command or proclamation issued by an authority.
37. **Emulate** NOUN following someone else's example.
38. **Effete** ADJECTIVE no longer productive; hence, lacking in or, worn out.
39. **Ephemeral** ADJECTIVE fleeting, temporary.
40. **Elicit** VERB to draw out.
41. **Exemplary** ADJECTIVE outstanding.
42. **Elucidate** VERB to make clear; to explain florid: ornate.
43. **Forbearance** NOUN patience, restraint.
44. **Facade** NOUN front or face, especially of a building.
45. **Fortuitous** ADJECTIVE lucky.
46. **Fallacious** ADJECTIVE unsound; misleading; deceptive.
47. **Fraught** NOUN filled with.
48. **Flaccid** ADJECTIVE lacking firmness.
49. **Ghastly** ADJECTIVE horrible, deathlike.
50. **Grimace** NOUN a distortion of the face to express an attitude or feeling.
51. **Hedonist** NOUN person who acts in pursuit of pleasure.
52. **Harbinger** NOUN a forerunner; ail announcer.
53. **Impetuous** ADJECTIVE rash, impulsive.

54. **Immaculate** ADJECTIVE spotless; pure.
55. **Inconsequential** ADJECTIVE without consequence, trivial, does not matter.
56. **Impeccable** ADJECTIVE faultless.
57. **Intrepid** ADJECTIVE fearless.
58. **Imprecation** NOUN a curse.
59. **Jubilation** NOUN extreme happiness, joy.
60. **Latent** ADJECTIVE hidden; present but not fully developed.
61. **Longevity** NOUN long (particularly long life).
62. **Maudlin** ADJECTIVE sentimental to the point of tears.
63. **Nonchalant** ADJECTIVE casual, calm, at ease.
64. **Oblivious** ADJECTIVE forgetful; absent-minded.
65. **Orator** NOUN speaker.
66. **Obviate** VERB to prevent, dispose of, or make unnecessary by appropriate actions.
67. **Parched** ADJECTIVE lacking water, dried up.
68. **Panacea** NOUN a remedy for all ills.
69. **Pragmatic** ADJECTIVE practical.
70. **Paraphrase** VERB to restate the meaning of a passage in other words.
71. **Pretentious** ADJECTIVE being self important, thinking you are better than others.
72. **Pecuniary** ADJECTIVE pertaining to money.
73. **Prosaic** ADJECTIVE ordinary.
74. **Pensive** ADJECTIVE sadly thoughtful.
75. **Provocative** ADJECTIVE causes a fuss, inflammatory, likely to get people riled up.
76. **Peruse** VERB to read carefully.
77. **Querulous** ADJECTIVE irritable, prone to argument.
78. **Radical** NOUN one who advocates extreme basic changes.
79. **Reclusive** ADJECTIVE hermit, withdrawn.
80. **Recapitulate** VERB to restate in a brief, concise form.
81. **Renovate** VERB to make new, being redone.
82. **Refute** VERB to prove incorrect or false.
83. **Reverence** NOUN deep respect.
84. **Sallow** ADJECTIVE sick.
85. **Scrutinize** VERB to look at carefully.
86. **Sanguinary** ADJECTIVE bloody.

87. **Spurious** ADJECTIVE false, untrue.
88. **Scourge** VERB to punish severely; to afflict; to whip.
89. **Substantiate** VERB to confirm, prove.
90. **Scrutinize** VERB to examine carefully.
91. **Superficial** ADJECTIVE shallow.
92. **Sleazy** ADJECTIVE flimsy and cheap.
93. **Surreptitious** ADJECTIVE secret.
94. **Tactful** ADJECTIVE polite.
95. **Tangible** ADJECTIVE real; actual.
96. **Transient** ADJECTIVE temporary, impermanent.
97. **Vanquish** VERB to subdue or conquer.
98. **Vindicate** VERB to free from blame.
99. **Wary** ADJECTIVE careful, watchful.
100. **Zenith** NOUN the highest point.

Word List 2 – Stem Words

Probably the best way of learning new vocabulary is our "two-for-one" strategy of learning a stem word and then you can recognize two, three or more words that use the stem word. If you are studying for an exam with a vocabulary section, this is the best strategy for you.

Below is an extensive list of stem words with their meaning and examples, followed by questions

A Root	Meaning	Examples
ab-, a-, abs-	away	absent, aversion
acr(i)-	sharp, pungent	acrid, acrimony
aer-, aero-	air, atmosphere	aeronautics, aerosol
agri-	field, country	agriculture,
amic-, imic-	friend	amicable, inimical
ant-, anti-	against, opposed to, preventive	antibiotic, antipodes
ante-, anti-	before, in front of, prior to	anticipate, antiquarian
anthropo-	human	anthropology, anthropomorphic
aqu-	water	aquarium, aqueduct
arche-, archi-	ruler	archangel, archetype
archaeo-, archeo-	ancient	archeology, archaic
arthr(o)-	joint	arthritis, arthropod
astr-, astro-	star, star-shaped	asterisk, astronomy
aud(i)-	hearing, listening, sound	auditorium, auditory
aut-, auto-	self; directed from within	automobile, autonomy
avi-	bird	aviary, aviation

B Root	Meaning	Example #1
	weight, pressure	barometer, barograph
basi-	at the bottom	basic, basis
bell(i)-	war	bellicose, belligerent
bibl-	book	bibliography, bible
bi(o)-	life	biology, biosphere
brev(i)-	brief, short (time)	abbreviation, brevity

C Root	Meaning	Examples
	glowing, iridescent	incandescent, candle
cap-, -cip-, capt-, -cept-	hold, take	capture, recipient
cardi(o)-	relating to the heart	cardiology, cardiograph
cav-	hollow	cavity, excavation
cent-	hundred	centennial, centurion
chloro-	green	chlorine, chlorophyll,
chron-	time	chronometer, chronology
circum-	around	circumference, circumcise
clar-	clear	clarity, declaration
clin-	bed, lean	Recline, inclined
cogn-	know	cognitive, recognize
contra-	against	contrast, contradict
cre-	make	creation, creature
cred-	believe, trust	credibility, credentials
cruc(i)-	cross	crucifix, crucify
crypt-	hidden	cryptic, cryptography
curr-, curs-	run	concurrent, recursion

cycl(o)-	circular	bicycle, cycle, cyclone

D Root	Meaning	Examples
de-	from, away from, removing	delete, demented
dens-	thick	condense, density
dent-	tooth	dental, dentures
	skin	dermis, epidermis
dorm-	sleep	dormant, dormitory

E Root	Meaning	Examples
equ-, -iqu-	even, level	equal, equivalence
ethn-	native	ethnicity, ethnic
eu-	well, good	euphoria, euthanasia
ex-, e-, ef-	from, out	exclude, extrude, extend
exter-, extra-	outer	exterior, extrasensory
extrem-	utmost, outermost	extremity, extremophile

F Root	Meaning	Examples
-fect-	make	defect, factory, manufacture
femin-	female	femininity, feminist
feder-	treaty, agreement, contract, league	confederation, federal
fend-, fens-	prevent	defend, offense
fid-, fis-	faith, trust	confidence, fidelity
fin-	end	finish, final
flig-, flict-	strike	conflict, inflict
flor-	flower	floral, florid
form-	shape	conformity, deformity
fract-, frag-	break	fracture, fragment
front-	forehead	confront, frontal
fug-, fugit-	flee	centrifuge, fugitive

G Root	Meaning	Examples
ger-, gest-	bear, carry	digest, gestation
glob-	sphere	global, globule
grad-, gress-	walk, step	grade, regress
gran-	grain	granary, granule
greg-	flock	gregarious, segregation

H Root	Meaning	Examples
haem-	blood	haemophilia, haemoglobin
hemi-	half	hemicycle, hemisphere
her-, hes-	cling	adhesive, coherent
hom(o)-	same	homosexual, homogenous
hort(i)-	garden	horticulture, horticulturist
hospit-	host	hospitality, hospitable
hydr(o)-	water	hydrophobia, hydroponic

I Root	Meaning	Examples
idi(o)-	personal	idiom, idiosyncrasy
ign-	fire	igneous, ignition
infra-	below, under	infrastructure, infrared
inter-	among, between	intermission, intersection

J Root	Meaning	Examples
jac- -ject-	cast, throw	eject, interject
jung-, junct-	join	conjunction, juncture
juven-	young, youth	juvenile, rejuvenate

K Root	Meaning	Examples
kil(o)-	thousand	kilobyte, kilogram, kilometer
kine-	movement, motion	Kinetic, kinesthetic

L Root	Meaning	Examples
lab-, laps-	slide, slip	elapse, relapse
lact-	milk	lactate, lactose
lax-	not tense	laxative, relaxation
leg-	law	legal, legislative
lev-	lift, light	elevator, levitation
liber-	free	liberation, liberty
lingu-	language, tongue	bilingual, linguistic
loc-	place	local, location
long-	long	elongate, longitude
lumin-	light	illumination, luminous
lun-	moon	lunar, lunatic

M Root	Meaning	Examples
maj-	greater	majesty, majority
mal-	bad	malicious, malignant
mania	mental illness	kleptomania, maniac
manu-	hand	manual, manuscript
mar-	sea	marine, maritime
maxim-	greatest	maximal, maximum
medi-, -midi-	middle	median, medieval
ment-	mind	demented, mentality
merc-	reward, wages	mercantile, merchant
merg-, mers-	dip, plunge	emerge, immersion
meter-, metr-	measure	metric, thermometer
micr(o)-	small	microphone, microscope
migr-	wander	emigrant, migrate
milit-	soldier	military, militia
mill-	thousand	millennium, million
mim-	repeat	mime, mimic
min-	less, smaller	minority, minuscule
mir-	wonder, amazement	admire, miracle
misce-, mixt-	mix	miscellaneous, mixture
mitt-, miss-	send	intermittent, transmission

M con't		
mon(o)-	one	monolith, monotone
mort-	death	immortal, mortuary
mov-, mot-	move	motion, momentum
mult(i)-	many, much	multiple, multiplex

N Root	Meaning	Examples
narc-	numb	narcosis, narcotic
nav-	ship	naval, navigate
neur-	nerve	neurology, neurosurgeon
nud-	naked	denude, nude
nutri	nourish	nutrition, nutrient

O Root	Meaning	Examples
ob-, o-, oc-, os-	against	obstinate, ostentatious
oct-	eight	octagon, octahedron
ocul-	eye	ocular, oculus
omni-	all	omnipotence, omnivore
opt-	eye	optical, optician
opt-	choose	adopt, optional
or-	mouth	oral, orator
ordin-	order	ordinal, ordinary
orn-	decorate	adorn, ornament
ov-	egg	oval, ovule

P Root	Meaning	Examples
pac-	peace	pacifism, pacifist
paed-, ped	child	pediatric, pediatrician
pall-	be pale	pallid, pallor
pand-, pans-	spread	expand, expansion
par(a)-	beside, near	parallel, parameter
past-	feed	pasture, repast
ped-	foot, child	pedal, quadruped
pharmac-	drug, medicine	pharmacy, pharmacist

P con't		
phob-	fear	hydrophobia, agoraphobia
phon(o)-	sound	microphone, phonograph
plan-	flat	planar, plane
plas-	mould	plasma, plastic
plaus-	clap	applaud, applause
pod-	foot	podiatry, tripod
pol-	pole	dipole, polar
pole-, poli-	city	metropolis, politics
port-	carry	export, transportation
post-	after, behind	posterior, postscript
pre-	before	prehistoric, previous
prim-	first	primary, primeval
priv(i)-	separate	deprivation, privilege
proxim-	nearest	approximate, proximity
pugn-	fight	pugnacious, repugnant

Q Root	Meaning	Examples
quadr-	four	quadrangle, quadrillion
	fifth	quintary, quintile
quot-	how many, how great	quota, quotient

R Root	Meaning	Examples
rad-, ras-	scrape, shave	abrade, abrasion
ranc-	rancidness, grudge, bitterness	rancid, rancour
re-, red-	again, back	recede, redact
retro-	backward, behind	retrograde, retrospective

R con't		
rid-, ris-	laugh	derision, ridicule
rod-, ros-	gnaw	erosion, rodent
rump-, rupt-	break	eruption, rupture

S Root	Meaning	Examples
sacr-, secr-	sacred	consecrate, sacrament
sanc-	holy	sanctify, sanctuary
sci-	know	prescient, science
scind-, sciss-	split	rescind, scissors
scrib-, script-	write	inscribe, scripture
se-, sed-	apart	secede, sedition
sect-, seg-	cut	section, segment
sed-	settle, calm	sedative, sedate
sema-	sign	semantics, semaphore
sen-	old man	senator, senility
sequ-, secut-	follow	consecutive, sequence
sign-	sign	design, designate
sist-	cause to stand	consist, persistence
soci-	group	associate, social
sol-	sun	solar
sol-	comfort	soothe, consolation
sol-	alone, only	sole, solo
solv-, solut-	loosen, set free	dissolve, solution
sorb-, sorpt-	suck	absorb, absorption
spec-, -spic-, spect-	look	conspicuous, inspection, specimen
spher-	ball	sphere, spheroid
squal-	scaly, dirty, filthy	squalid, squalor
statu-, -stitu-	stand	institution, statute
stell-	star	constellation, stellar
still-	drip	distillation
stinct-	apart	distinction, distinguish

S con't		
stru-, struct-	structure, building	construction, construe
subter-	under	subterfuge, subterranean
sum-, sumpt-	take	assumption, consume

T Root	Meaning	Examples
tac-, -tic-	be silent	reticent, tacit
tang-, -ting-, tact-, tag-	touch	contact, tactile
tele-	far, end	telegram, telephone
tempor-	time	contemporary, temporal
ten-, -tin-, tent-	hold	detention, tenacious
tend-, tens-	stretch	extend, extension
termin-	boundary, limit, end	terminal, termination
terr-	dry land	terrace, terrain
test-	witness	testament, testimony
tex-, text-	weave	texture, textile
tot-	all, whole	total, totality
trans-, tra-, tran-	across	tradition, transportation
traum-	wound	trauma, traumatic
tri-	three	triad, tripod
tri-	three	triangle, trivia
typ-	stamp, model	archetype, typography

U Root	Meaning	Examples
ultim-	farthest	ultimatum, ultimate
ut-, us-	use	usual, utility

V Root	Meaning	Examples
vac-	empty	vacancy, vacuum
vad-, vas-	go	evade, pervasive
vag-	wander	vague, vagabond
vap-	lack (of)	evaporation, vapid
ven-, vent-	come	advent, convention
vend-	sell	vendor, vending
verb-	word	verbal, verbatim
vert-, vers-	turn	convert, invert
veter-	old	inveterate, veteran
vi-	way	deviate, via
vid-, vis-	see	video, vision
vil-	cheap	vile, vilify
vinc-, vict-	conquer	invincible, victory
viv-	live	revive, survive, vivid
voc-	voice	vocal, provocative
volv-, volut-	roll	convolution, revolve
vor-, vorac-	swallow	devour, voracious

Z Root	Meaning	Examples
zo-	animal, living being	zoo, zoology

Stem Words Practice Questions

1. Choose the meaning of the stem word quot-

   a. How many
   b. Development
   c. Field
   d. Government

2. Choose the meaning of the stem word stu-

   a. Health study
   b. Building
   c. Stretched out
   d. On both sides

3. Choose the meaning of the stem word baro-

   a. Weight or pressure
   b. North
   c. Brief
   d. Greatness

4. Choose the meaning of the stem word bibl-

   a. At the bottom
   b. Deep
   c. Book
   d. Wood

5. Choose the meaning of the stem word vac-

   a. Pretty
   b. Stone
   c. Empty
   d. Vault

6. Choose the meaning of the stem word cand-

   a. Long
   b. Goat like
   c. Harden
   d. Glowing

7. Choose the meaning of the stem word temin-

   a. End
   b. Tenth part
   c. Leadership
   d. Move away from

8. Choose the meaning of the stem word derm-

   a. Above
   b. Skin
   c. Insane actions
   d. Fingers

9. Choose the meaning of the stem word equ-

   a. Even or level
   b. Knowledge
   c. Inside or within
   d. House

10. Choose the meaning of the stem word haem-

    a. Mental state

    b. Blood

    c. Child health

    d. Time

11. Choose the meaning of the stem word hemi-

    a. Half

    b. Air

    c. Strange

    d. Foreign

12. Choose the meaning of the stem word infra-

    a. Doubtful

    b. Foundation

    c. Strength

    d. Below or under

13. Choose the meaning of the stem word junct-

    a. Sound

    b. Join

    c. Jungle

    d. Electricity

14. Choose the meaning of the stem word lact-

    a. Shine

    b. Milk

    c. Lecture

    d. Teaching

15. Choose the meaning of the stem word lingu-

   a. Teacher
   b. Language, tongue
   c. Knowledge
   d. Tribes

16. Choose the meaning of the stem word nav-

   a. Slime
   b. Ship
   c. Join
   d. Tell

17. Choose the meaning of the stem word pac-

   a. Feed
   b. Ancient
   c. Peace
   d. Maiden

18. Choose the meaning of the stem word retro-

   a. Backward or behind
   b. Air less
   c. Kidney
   d. Nose or snout

19. Choose the meaning of the stem word rupt-

   a. Gnaw
   b. Prow
   c. Throat
   d. Break

20. Choose the meaning of the stem word sacr-

a. Sacred
b. Flesh
c. Scratch
d. Seriousness

21. Choose the meaning of the stem word termin-

a. God
b. Machine
c. Boundary or end
d. Weave

22. Choose the meaning of the stem word ultim-

a. Fruitful
b. Farthest
c. Infection
d. Shadow

23. Choose the meaning of the stem word ten-

a. Sacred
b. Flesh
c. Scratch
d. Hold

24. Choose the meaning of the stem word vi-

a. God
b. Way
c. Boundary or end
d. Weave

25. Choose the meaning of the stem word privi-
   a. Fruitful
   b. Farthest
   c. Infection
   d. Separate

ANSWER KEY – PART I

1. A
The stem word quot- means how many, for example quota.

2. B
The stem word stu- means building, for example construction.

3. A
The stem word baro- means relating to weight or pressure, for example barometer.

4. C
The stem word bibl- relates to books, for example bibliography and bible.

5. C
The stem word vac- means empty, for example vacancy.

6. D
The stem word cand- means glowing, for examples candle and candid.

7. A
The stem word termin- means end, for example terminal.

8. B
The stem word derm- relates to skin, for example dermis and epidermis.

9. A
The stem word ecu- means even or level, for example equal.

10. B
The stem word haem- means blood, for example hemophilia.

11. A
The stem word hemi- means half, for example hemisphere.

12. D
The stem word infra- means below and under, for example infrastructure.

13. B
The stem word junct- means join, for example junction.

14. B
The stem word lact- means milk, for example lactate.

15. B
The stem word lingu- means relating to language, tongue, for example bilingual and linguistic.

16. B
The stem word nav- means ship, for example naval.

17. C
The stem word pac- means peace, for example pact and pacify.

18. A
The stem word retro- means backward or behind, for example retrospect and retrograde.

19. D
The stem word rupt- means break, for example rupture.

20. A
The stem word sacr- means sacred, for example consecrate and sacrament.

21. C
The stem word termin- means boundary or end, for examples termination and terminal.

22. B
The stem word ultim- means farthest, for example ultimate.

23. D
The stem word ten- means hold, for example detention.

24. B

The stem word vi- means way, for example via.

25. D

The stem word privi- means separate, for example privilege.

Answer Sheet

	A	B	C	D	E		A	B	C	D	E
1	○	○	○	○	○	21	○	○	○	○	○
2	○	○	○	○	○	22	○	○	○	○	○
3	○	○	○	○	○	23	○	○	○	○	○
4	○	○	○	○	○	24	○	○	○	○	○
5	○	○	○	○	○	25	○	○	○	○	○
6	○	○	○	○	○						
7	○	○	○	○	○						
8	○	○	○	○	○						
9	○	○	○	○	○						
10	○	○	○	○	○						
11	○	○	○	○	○						
12	○	○	○	○	○						
13	○	○	○	○	○						
14	○	○	○	○	○						
15	○	○	○	○	○						
16	○	○	○	○	○						
17	○	○	○	○	○						
18	○	○	○	○	○						
19	○	○	○	○	○						
20	○	○	○	○	○						

Stem Words Practice Part II

1. Choose the stem word that means air or atmosphere.

   a. Bran-

   b. Gen-

   c. Aero-

   d. Agog-

2. Choose the stem word that means women, female.

   a. Fam-

   b. Ward-

   c. Gust-

   d. Femin-

3. Choose the stem word that means end.

   a. Gran-

   b. Fin-

   c. Flux-

   d. Eur-

4. Choose the stem word that means life.

   a. Bio-

   b. Calcu-

   c. Ext-

   d. Ago-

5. Choose the stem word that means outermost, utmost.

   a. Frug-

   b. Etym-

   c. Larg-

   d. Extrem-

6. Choose the stem word that means at the bottom.

    a. Trid-
    b. Eco-
    c. Basi-
    d. Ful-

7. Choose the stem word that means host.

    a. Hospit-
    b. Habi-
    c. Proc-
    d. Paci-

8. Choose the stem word that means people, race, tribe, nation.

    a. Adul-
    b. Baro-
    c. Cad-
    d. Ethn-

9. Choose the stem word that means idea; thought.

    a. Cupl(u)-
    b. Stat-
    c. Ide(o)-
    d. Anal-

10. Choose the stem word that means among, between.

    a. Chang-
    b. Sta-
    c. Inter-
    d. Less-

11. **Choose the stem word that means young, youth.**

    a. Juven-
    b. Yot-
    c. Drap-
    d. Rabi-

12. **Choose the stem word that means not tense.**

    a. Hommi-
    b. Lax-
    c. –Tic
    d. Tens-

13. **Choose the stem word that means mental illness.**

    a. Kilm-
    b. Cher-
    c. Mania-
    d. Logy-

14. **Choose the stem word that means greater.**

    a. Cede-
    b. Culp-
    c. Maj-
    d. Lar-

15. **Choose the stem word that means light.**

    a. Lumin-
    b. Radi-
    c. Scope-
    d. Promu-

16. Choose the stem word that means eight.

    a. Kine-

    b. Zeb-

    c. Oct-

    d. Puin-

17. Choose the stem word that means movement, motion.

    a. Kis-

    b. Kine-

    c. Trid-

    d. Agog-

18. Choose the stem word that means child.

    a. Dropi-

    b. Calp-

    c. Ped-

    d. Small-

19. Choose the stem word that means fifth.

    a. Quint-

    b. Ward-

    c. Caldi-

    d. Scor-

20. Choose the stem word that means empty.

    a. Odor-

    b. Vac-

    c. Mar-

    d. Nema-

21. Choose the stem word that means animal, living being.

   a. Ery-

   b. Brat(o)-

   c. Anis-

   d. Zo-

22. Choose the stem word that means before.

   a. Hered-

   b. Pre-

   c. Part-

   d. Jug-

23. Choose the stem word that means end.

   a. Grou-

   b. Stari-

   c. Fin-

   d. Ladi-

24. Choose the stem word that means word.

   a. Nauti-

   b. Baro-

   c. Justi-

   d. Verb-

25. Choose the stem word that means sphere.

   a. Curv-

   b. Glob-

   c. Blob-

   d. Derog-

STEM WORD ANSWER KEY PART II

1. C

The stem root word aero- means air, atmosphere, for example, aeronautics and aerosol.

2. D

The stem root word femin- means relating to women, female, for example femininity.

3. B

The stem root word fin-means end, for example finish and final.

4. A

The stem root word bi(o)- means life, for example, biology, biologist and biosphere.

5. D

The stem root word extrem- means outermost, utmost, for example extremity.

6. C

The stem root word basi- means at the bottom, for example basic and basis.

7. A

The stem root word hospit- means host, for example hospitality.

8. D

The stem root word ethn- means people, race, tribe, nation, for example ethnic and ethnicity.

9. C

The stem root word ide(o)- means idea or thought, for example ideogram and ideology.

10. C

The stem root word inter- means among or between, for example intercollegiate, intermission and intersection.

11. A
The stem root word juven- means young or youth, for example juvenile, rejuvenate.

12. B
The stem root word lax- means not tense, for example laxative and relaxation.

13. C
The stem root word mania- means relating to mental illness, for example kleptomania and maniac.

14. C
The stem root word maj- means greater, for example majesty, majority.

15. A
The stem root word lumin- means light, for example illumination and luminous.

16. C
The stem root word oct- means eight, for example octagon and octahedron.

17. B
The stem root word kine- means air movement, motion, for example telekinesis, kinetic energy and kinesthetic.

18. C
The stem root word ped- means child, for example pedagogy.

19. A
The stem root word quint- means fifth, for example quinary and quintet.

20. B
The stem root word vac- means empty, for example vacancy, vacation and vacuum.

21. D
The stem root word zo- means animal, living being, for example, protozoa, zoo and zoology.

22. B

The stem root word pre- means before, for example previous.

23. C

The stem root word fin- means relating to end, for example finish and final.

24. D

The stem root word verb- means relating to word, for example verbal, verbatim, verbosity.

25. B

The stem root word glob- means relating to sphere, for example global and globule.

Word List 3 – Most Common Prefix

A prefix is a word part at the beginning of a word which helps create the meaning. Understanding prefix is a powerful tool for increasing your vocabulary because many prefix are used by two, three or more words. The word prefix contains a prefix "pre-," which means before. If you know the meaning of the prefix, you can guess the meaning of the word, even if you are not familiar with the word.

Prefix may have more than one meaning. Here is a list of 100 commonly used prefixes along with their meaning and an example of their use.

Study the list below and then answer the questions below.

Prefix	Meaning	Example
a-, an-	without	Amoral, amateur
acro-	high up	acropolis, acrobat
ab-	away	abduction, abstain
anti-	against	antidote, antivirus, antifreeze
com-, con-	together	conference, confer
contra-, contro	against, opposite	contradiction, contraception
crypto-	hidden	cryptography
demo-	people, nation	demographics
extra-	more than	extracurricular, extramural
hyper-	over, more	hyperactive
homo-	same	homonym, homosexual
im-, ir-, il-, in-	not, without	illegal, inconsiderate,
inter-	between	Intersect, interstate
intra	within	intramural, intranet
intro-	in, into	Introspect, introduction
multi-	many	multimillionaire, multiple
mis-	bad, wrong	miscarriage
micro-	small, million	microscope, microgram
micro-	one millionth	microgram, microeconomics
mal-, mis	bad	maladjusted, malware, mistake

mini-	small	miniskirt, miniscule
multi	many	multiple, multiplicity
non-	not, without	Nonentity, nonconformist
omni-	all, every	omniscient, omnivore
octa	eight	octagon, octopus
pre-	before	preview, precedent
penta-	five	pentagon
pro-	in favor of	pro-choice, promotion
poly-	many	polygon, polyglot
quadr-, quart-	four	quadrangle, quadruple
retro-	backward	retrospect, retro
sub-	under	submarine, subterranean
semi-	half	semi-automatic , semi-
super-	extremely	superhuman, supernatural
tele-	long distance	Telephoto, telecommunication
thermo	heat	thermos
tri-	three	triangle, tricolor
thermo	heat	thermometer
un-	not, opposite	unconstitutional
uni-	one, single	unification
ultra	beyond	ultraviolet
zoo-	relating to animals	zoology

PREFIX ANSWER SHEET

	A	B	C	D	E		A	B	C	D	E
1	○	○	○	○	○	21	○	○	○	○	○
2	○	○	○	○	○	22	○	○	○	○	○
3	○	○	○	○	○	23	○	○	○	○	○
4	○	○	○	○	○	24	○	○	○	○	○
5	○	○	○	○	○	25	○	○	○	○	○
6	○	○	○	○	○						
7	○	○	○	○	○						
8	○	○	○	○	○						
9	○	○	○	○	○						
10	○	○	○	○	○						
11	○	○	○	○	○						
12	○	○	○	○	○						
13	○	○	○	○	○						
14	○	○	○	○	○						
15	○	○	○	○	○						
16	○	○	○	○	○						
17	○	○	○	○	○						
18	○	○	○	○	○						
19	○	○	○	○	○						
20	○	○	○	○	○						

Prefix Questions

1. Choose the prefix that means single or uniform.

    a. Uni-

    b. Epic-

    c. Hydra-

    d. Si-

2. Choose the prefix that means long distance.

    a. Mini-

    b. Tele-

    c. Dis-

    d. Sci-

3. Choose the prefix that means bad.

    a. Bathy-

    b. Mal-

    c. Re-

    d. Ectos-

4. Choose the prefix that means all or every.

    a. Multi-

    b. Omni-

    c. Creo-

    d. Mal-

5. Choose the prefix that means opposite and against.

   a. Contra-

   b. Deg-

   c. Erg-

   d. Re-

6. Choose the prefix that means wrong or bad.

   a. Dis-

   b. Demo-

   c. Grad-

   d. Mis-

7. Choose the prefix that means many.

   a. Poly-

   b. Pro-

   c. Pan-

   d. Recti-

8. Choose the prefix that means before.

   a. Anti

   b. Tachy-

   c. Pre-

   d. Quin-

9. Choose the best meaning of the prefix anti.

   a. Water

   b. Enemies

   c. Against

   d. Missing the mark

10. Choose the best meaning of the prefix thermo.

    a. Long distance

    b. Heat

    c. Hard

    d. Pressure

11. Choose the best meaning of the prefix intra.

    a. Square shape

    b. Between

    c. Round

    d. Border line

12. Choose the best meaning of the prefix multi.

    a. Blood

    b. Severe pain

    c. Narrow

    d. Many

13. Choose the best meaning of the prefix mini.

    a. Harsh

    b. Acute

    c. Small

    d. Larger than normal

14. Choose the best meaning of the prefix octa.

    a. Extreme

    b. Eight

    c. Short

    d. Water animal

How to Improve your Vocabulary

15. Choose the best meaning of the prefix pro.

a. Extremely cold

b. Before

c. In favor of

d. Repeat

16. Choose the best meaning of the prefix quad.

a. 3-Sided

b. Four

c. Five

d. Many sided

17. Choose the best meaning of the prefix retro.

a. Related to temperature

b. Against

c. Deny

d. Backward

18. Choose the best meaning of the prefix semi.

a. Half

b. Complete

c. Related to money

d. Related to weapons

19. Choose the best meaning of the prefix ultra.

a. Double

b. Far beyond

c. Slow

d. Related to health

20. Choose the best meaning of the prefix tri.

   a. Three

   b. Acrobat

   c. Related to time

   d. Related to air

21. Choose the best meaning of the prefix un.

   a. Alone

   b. Together

   c. Opposite

   d. Agreement

22. Choose the best meaning of the prefix zoo.

   a. Same time

   b. Relating to animals

   c. Related to the forest

   d. Large house

23. Choose the best meaning of the prefix homo.

   a. Same

   b. Red in color

   c. Related to blood

   d. Hard

24. Choose the best meaning of the prefix super.

   a. Extremely

   b. Relating to animals

   c. Related to the forest

   d. Large house

25. Choose the best meaning of the prefix intro.

   a. Same

   b. Red in color

   c. Into

   d. Hard

ANSWER KEY

1. A
The prefix uni means single and uniform, for example unification.

2. B
The prefix tele means long distance, for example telecommunication.

3. B
The prefix mal means bad, for example maladjusted.

4. B
The prefix omni means all or every, for example omniscient.

5. A
The prefix contra means opposite or against, for example contradiction.

6. D
The prefix mis means wrong or bad, for example misstep or miscarriage.

7. A
The prefix poly means many, for example polygon.

8. C
The prefix pre means before, for example preview.

9. C
The prefix anti means against, for example, antichrist.

10. B
The prefix thermo means heat, for example thermostat.

11. B
The prefix intra means between, for example intravenous.

12. D
The prefix multi means many, for example multiple.

13. C
The prefix mini means small, for example miniscule.

14. B
The prefix octa means eight, for example octagon.

15. C
The prefix pro means in favor of, for example promotion.

16. B
The prefix quad means four, for example quadruped, or four legs.

17. D
The prefix retro means backward, for example retrospect.

18. A
The prefix semi means half, for example semi-detached.

19. B
The prefix ultra means far beyond, for example ultraviolet.

20. A
The prefix tri means three, for example trilogy.

21. C
The prefix un means opposite and not, for example unconstitutional.

22. B
The prefix zoo means animal, for example zoology.

23. A
The prefix homo means same, for example homosexual.

24. A
The prefix super means extreme, for example supernatural.

25. C
The prefix intro means into, for example introspect.

Word List 4 – Most Common Synonyms

Synonyms, like prefix and stem words are a great two-for-one strategy for improving your vocabulary fast. Below is a list of the most common synonyms followed by 30 questions.

Word	Synonym	Synonym
Amazing	Extraordinary	Astonishing
Aggravate	Infuriate	Annoy
Arrogant	Imperious	Disdainful
Answer	Respond	Reply
Antagonist	Enemy	Adversary
Attain	Achieve	Reach
Benevolence	Kindness	Charitable
Berate	Disapprove	Criticize
Beautiful	Gorgeous	Attractive
Big	Gigantic	Enormous
	Loud	Rowdy
Boring	Uninteresting	Dull
Budget	Plan	Allot
Contradict	Oppose	Deny
Category	Division	Classification
Complete	Comprehensive	Total
	Prominent	Bold
Catch	Seize	Capture
Chubby	Fat	Plump
Congenial	Pleasant	Friendly
Criticize	Berate	Belittle
Delicious	Delectable	Appetizing
Describe	Portray	Picture
Destroy	Ruin	Wreck
Dwindle	Diminish	Abate
Difference	Contrast	Dissimilarity
Decay	Rot	Decompose
Decent	Pure	Honorable
Decipher	Decode	Decrypt
Eager	Enthusiastic	Willing

Word	Synonym	Synonym
Elaborate	Enhance	Explain
Explain	Elaborate	Elucidate
Eccentric	Weird	Odd
Embezzle	Misappropriate	Steal
Fastidious	Exacting	Particular
Flatter	Praise	Compliment
Fantasy	Imagine	Day dream
	Caress	Stroke
Furious	Raging	Angry
Good	Sound	Excellent
Genuine	Real	Actual
Gay	Happy	Cheerful
Ghastly	Horrible	Gruesome
Handicap	Disadvantage	Disability
Haughty	Proud	Arrogant
Hypocrisy	Pretense	Duplicity
Humiliate	Shame	Humble
	Unconquerable	Indomitable
Interesting	Captivating	Engaging
Illicit	Illegal	Unlawful
Immaterial	Irrelevant	Unimportant
Illustrious	Famous	Noble
Impregnable	Unconquerable	Unbeatable
Incoherent	Jumbled	Confused
Dishonest	Deceitful	Duplicitous
Itinerary	Schedule	Route
Intrusive	Invasive	Nosy
Jargon	Slang	Lingo
Jovial	Jolly	Genial
Juvenile	Immature	Adolescent
Justification	Reason	Excuse
Justification	Scoff	Mock
Jostle	Shove	Push
Keep	Hold	Retain
Keen	Sharp	Acute
Keel	Swagger	Reel
Look	Gaze	Inspect
Little	Tiny	Small

Word	Synonym	Synonym
Limitation	Constraint	Boundary
Least	Lowest	Minimum
Malice	Bitterness	Spite
Match	Identical	Correspond
Memorial	Commemorate	Monument
Meager	Bare	Scanty
Memento	Gift	Keepsake
Necessary	Required	Essential
Negotiate	Scheme	Bargain
Novice	Learner	Beginner
Narrate	Disclose	Tell
Negligible	Unimportant	Insignificant
Obstinate	Adamant	Stubborn
Omen	Premonition	Foreboding
Opulence	Abundance	Wealth
Omit	Exclude	Disregard
Perplex	Confuse	Astonish
Parcel	Bundle	Package
Pause	Wait	Break
Plight	Situation	Scenario
Quack	Fake	Charlatan
Quip	Joke	Jest
Renown	Famous	Popular
Radiate	Emanate	Effuse
Run	Accelerate	Dash
Romantic	Amorous	Loving
Rebel	Dissent	Renegade
Reconcile	Harmonize	Conciliate
Render	Give	Present
Sanction	Authorize	Approve
Satisfy	Sate	Gratify
Strong	Powerful	Hard
Sealed	Stroll	Walk
Shackle	Retrain	Confine
Saunter	Shut	Close
Terminate	End	Finish
True	Accurate	Factual
Thrive	Prosper	Progress

Word	Synonym	Synonym
Tumult	Confusion	Disturbance
Tacit	Implicit	Implied
Terminate	End	Finish
Thaw	Unfreeze	Defrost
Update	Modernize	Renew
Ultimate	Supreme	Eventual
Uncanny	Mysterious	Spooky
Valid	Accurate	Legitimate
Verify	Validate	Certify
Vacate	Quit	Resign
Various	Assortment	Diverse
Wrath	Rage	Fury
Weird	Strange	Odd
Yearly	Annually	Year by year
Yank	Pull	Draw
Yearn	Long for	Desire
Zealous	Enthusiastic	Dedicated
Zoom	Speed off	Hurry

SYNONYM PRACTICE QUESTION ANSWER SHEET

	A	B	C	D	E		A	B	C	D	E
1	○	○	○	○	○	21	○	○	○	○	○
2	○	○	○	○	○	22	○	○	○	○	○
3	○	○	○	○	○	23	○	○	○	○	○
4	○	○	○	○	○	24	○	○	○	○	○
5	○	○	○	○	○	25	○	○	○	○	○
6	○	○	○	○	○						
7	○	○	○	○	○						
8	○	○	○	○	○						
9	○	○	○	○	○						
10	○	○	○	○	○						
11	○	○	○	○	○						
12	○	○	○	○	○						
13	○	○	○	○	○						
14	○	○	○	○	○						
15	○	○	○	○	○						
16	○	○	○	○	○						
17	○	○	○	○	○						
18	○	○	○	○	○						
19	○	○	○	○	○						
20	○	○	○	○	○						

Synonym Practice Questions

1. Select the synonym of conspicuous.

    a. Important

    b. Prominent

    c. Beautiful

    d. Convincing

2. Select the synonym of benevolence.

    a. Happiness

    b. Courage

    c. Kindness

    d. Loyalty

3. Select the synonym of boisterous.

    a. Loud

    b. Soft

    c. Gentle

    d. Warm

4. Select the synonym of fondle.

    a. Hold

    b. Caress

    c. Throw

    d. Keep

5. Select the synonym of impregnable.

    a. Unconquerable

    b. Impossible

    c. Unlimited

    d. Imperfect

6. Select the synonym of antagonist.

    a. Supporter

    b. Fan

    c. Enemy

    d. Partner

7. Select the synonym of memento.

    a. Monument

    b. Remembrance

    c. Gift

    d. Idea

8. Select the synonym of insidious.

    a. Wise

    b. Brave

    c. Helpful

    d. Deceitful

9. Select the synonym of itinerary.

    a. Schedule

    b. Guidebook

    c. Pass

    d. Diary

10. Select the synonym of illustrious.

    a. Rich

    b. Noble

    c. Gallant

    d. Poor

11. Select the pair below that are synonyms.

   a. Jargon and Slang

   b. Slander and Plagiarism

   c. Devotion and Devout

   d. Current and Outdated

12. Select the pair below that are synonyms.

   a. Render and Give

   b. Recognition and Cognizant

   c. Stem and Root

   d. Adjust and Redo

13. Select the pair below that are synonyms.

   a. Private and Public

   b. Intrusive and Invasive

   c. Mysterious and Unknown

   d. Common and Unique

14. Select the pair below that are synonyms.

   a. Renowned and Popular

   b. Guard and Safe

   c. Aggressive and Shy

   d. Curtail and Avoid

15. Select the pair below that are synonyms.

   a. Brevity and Ambiguous

   b. Fury and Light-hearted

   c. Incoherent and Jumbled

   d. Benign And Malignant

16. Select the pair below that are synonyms.

    a. Congenial and Pleasant

    b. Distort and Similar

    c. Valuable and Rich

    d. Asset and Liability

17. Select the pair below that are synonyms.

    a. Circumstance and Plan

    b. Negotiate and Scheme

    c. Ardent and Whimsical

    d. Plight and Situation

18. Select the pair below that are synonyms.

    a. Berate and Criticize

    b. Unspoken and Unknown

    c. Tenet and Favor

    d. Turf and Seashore

19. Select the pair below that are synonyms.

    a. Adequate and Inadequate

    b. Sate and Satisfy

    c. Sufficient and Lacking

    d. Spectator and Teacher

20. Select the pair below that are synonyms.

    a. Pensive and Alibi

    b. Terminate and End

    c. Plot and Point

    d. Jaded and Honest

CHOOSE THE SYNONYM OF THE UNDERLINED WORD

21. I cannot wait to try some of the <u>delectable</u> dishes served in the new restaurant.

    a. Unique

    b. Expensive

    c. New

    d. Delicious

22. Can you <u>describe</u> the character of Juliet in the play?

    a. Report

    b. Portray

    c. State

    d. Draw

23. The soldiers <u>destroyed</u> the rebel's camp.

    a. Ruined

    b. Ended

    c. Fixed

    d. Conquered

24. There is a big <u>difference</u> in Esther Pete's grades.

    a. Complication

    b. Dissimilarity

    c. Minus

    d. Increase

25. I can <u>attain</u> my goals in life when I study hard.

    a. Finish

    b. Forget

    c. Effect

    d. Achieve

26. The lecture was so <u>boring</u> everybody was starting to get sleepy.

    a. Uninteresting

    b. Sensible

    c. Fast

    d. Exciting

27. The <u>eager</u> crowd yelled and cheered for their favorite team during the basketball tournament.

    a. Bored

    b. Uninterested

    c. Angry

    d. Enthusiastic

28. The government is planning to <u>end</u> famine through mass food production.

    a. Close

    b. Avoid

    c. Stop

    d. Start

29. Children <u>enjoy</u> playing in the park with their playmates.

    a. Dislike

    b. Relish

    c. Spend

    d. Uninterested

30. Can you <u>elaborate</u> on the reason behind your tardiness?

    a. Define

    b. Correct

    c. Explain

    d. Interpret

SYNONYM PRACTICE ANSWER KEY

1. B
Conspicuous and prominent are synonyms.

2. C
Benevolence and kindness are synonyms.

3. A
Boisterous and loud are synonyms.

4. B
Fondle and caress are synonyms.

5. A
Impregnable and unconquerable are synonyms.

6. C
Antagonist and enemy are synonyms.

7. C
Memento and gift are synonyms.

8. D
Insidious and deceitful are synonyms.

9. A
Itinerary and schedule are synonyms.

10. B
Illustrious and noble are synonyms.

11. A
Jargon and slang are synonyms.

12. A
Render and give are synonyms.

13. B
Intrusive and invasive are synonyms.

14. A
Renowned and popular are synonyms.

15. C
Incoherent and jumbled are synonyms.

16. A
Congenial and pleasant are synonyms.

17. D
Plight and situation are synonyms.

18. A
Berate and criticize are synonyms.

19. B
Sate and satisfy are synonyms.

20. B
Terminate and end are synonyms.

21. D
Delectable and delicious are synonyms.

22. B
Describe and portray are synonyms.

23. A
Destroy and ruin are synonyms.

24. B
Difference and dissimilarity are synonyms.

25. D
Attain and achieve are synonyms.

26. A
Boring and uninteresting are synonyms.

27. D
Eager and enthusiastic are synonyms.

28. C
End and stop are synonyms.

29. B
Enjoy and relish are synonyms.

30. C
Elaborate and explain are synonyms.

Word List 5 – Most Common Antonyms

Antonyms, like synonyms and stems, are a great two-for-one strategy for increasing your vocabulary. Below is a list of the most common antonyms, following by practice questions.

Word	Antonym	Antonym
Abundant	Scarce	Insufficient
Abnormal	Standard	Normal
Advance	Retreat	Recoil
Aimless	Directed	Motivated
Absurd	Sensible	Wise
Authentic	Imitation	Fake
Benevolence	Animosity	Indifference
Bloodless	Sensitive	Feeling
Blissful	Miserable	Sorrowful
Brilliant	Dulled	Dark
Certainty	Uncertainty	Doubtful
Capable	Inept	Incompetent
Cease	Begin	Commence
Charge	Discharge	Exonerate
Cohesive	Weak	Yielding
Console	Aggravate	Annoy
Confused	Enlightened	Attentive
Captivity	Liberty	Freedom
Diligent	Negligent	Languid
Dreadful	Pleasant	Pleasing
Decisive	Procrastinating	Indecisive
Deranged	Sane	Sensible
Disable	Enable	Assist
Discord	Harmony	Cooperation
Disjointed	Connected	Attached
Dogmatic	Flexible	Amenable
Erratic	Consistent	Dependable
Ecstatic	Despaired	Tormented
Eligible	Improper	Unfit
Escalate	Diminish	Decrease

Word	Antonym	Antonym
Elusive	Confronting	Attracting
Exhibit	Conceal	Hide
Fidelity	Disloyalty	Infidelity
Factual	Imprecise	Incorrect
Fearful	Courageous	Brave
Famous	Obscure	Unknown
Gaunt	Plump	Thick
Graceful	Awkward	Careless
Goodness	Meanness	Wickedness
Glamorous	Irritating	Offensive
Hard	Soft	Pliable
Hoarse	Smooth	Pleasing
Hidden	Bare	Exposed
Hearty	Apathetic	Lethargic
Harmful	Harmless	Safe
Harsh	Mild	Gentle
Idiotic	Smart	Intelligent
Idle	Busy	Working
Illegal	Lawful	Authorized
Illicit	Legal	Lawful
Illuminate	Obfuscate	Confuse
Immense	Tiny	Small
Intimate	Formal	Unfriendly
Identical	Opposite	Different
Immense	Minute	Tiny
Justice	Lawlessness	Unfairness
Jealous	Content	Trusting
Joyful	Sorrowful	Sad
Jumpy	Composed	Collected
Knack	Inability	Ineptitude
Kill	Create	Bear
Keen	Uninterested	Reluctant
Laughable	Serious	Grave
Latter	Former	First
Legible	Unreadable	Unclear
Literal	Figurative	Metaphorical
Loathe	Love	Like
Legendary	Factual	True

Word	Antonym	Antonym
Large	Little	Small
Miserable	Cheerful	Joyful
Moderate	Excessive	Unrestrained
Magical	Boring	Ordinary
Minor	Major	Significant
Myriad	Few	Scant
Narrow	Broad	Wide
Nasty	Pleasant	Magnificent
Nimble	Awkward	Clumsy
Optional	Compulsory	Required
Operational	Inactive	Inoperative
Optimistic	Pessimistic	Doubtful
Ordinary	Abnormal	Uncommon
Pester	Delight	Please
Penalize	Forgive	Reward
Placate	Agitate	Upset
Practical	Unfeasible	Unrealistic
Pensive	Shallow	Ignorant
Queasy	Comfortable	Satisfied
Quietly	Loudly	Audibly
Quirky	Conventional	Normal
Qualified	Unqualified	Incapable
Rapid	Slow	Leisurely
Refuse	Agree	Assent
Reluctant	Enthusiastic	Excited
Romantic	Realistic	Pragmatic
Ridicule	Flatter	Praise
Refresh	Damage	Ruin
Rough	Level	Smooth
Sacrifice	Refuse	Hold
Sadistic	Humane	Kind
Sane	Deranged	Insane
Save	Spend	Splurge
Scarce	Abundant	Plenty
Scorn	Approve	Delight
Scatter	Gather	Collect
Shrink	Expand	Grow
Simple	Complex	Complicated

Word	Antonym	Antonym
Stingy	Generous	Bountiful
Sterile	Dirty	Infected
Tedious	Interesting	Exciting
Tactful	Indiscreet	Careless
Tough	Weak	Vulnerable
Transparent	Opaque	Cloudy
Terminate	Initiate	Start
Truth	Lie	Untruth
Understand	Misunderstand	Misinterpret
Usable	Useless	Unfit
Validate	Veto	Reject
Vanquish	Endorse	Surrender
Vanish	Appear	Materialize
Vicious	Gentle	Nice
Vice	Virtue	Propriety
Villain	Hero	Savior
Vulnerable	Strong	Powerful
Wary	Reckless	Careless
Wasteful	Frugal	Thrifty
Wane	Grow	Increase
Weary	Lively	Energetic
Young	Old	Mature
Yonder	Nearby	Close
Zealous	Lethargic	Unenthusiastic

Antonym Practice Answer Sheet

	A	B	C	D	E			A	B	C	D	E
1	○	○	○	○	○		21	○	○	○	○	○
2	○	○	○	○	○		22	○	○	○	○	○
3	○	○	○	○	○		23	○	○	○	○	○
4	○	○	○	○	○		24	○	○	○	○	○
5	○	○	○	○	○		25	○	○	○	○	○
6	○	○	○	○	○		26	○	○	○	○	○
7	○	○	○	○	○		27	○	○	○	○	○
8	○	○	○	○	○		28	○	○	○	○	○
9	○	○	○	○	○		29	○	○	○	○	○
10	○	○	○	○	○		30	○	○	○	○	○
11	○	○	○	○	○							
12	○	○	○	○	○							
13	○	○	○	○	○							
14	○	○	○	○	○							
15	○	○	○	○	○							
16	○	○	○	○	○							
17	○	○	○	○	○							
18	○	○	○	○	○							
19	○	○	○	○	○							
20	○	○	○	○	○							

Antonym Practice Questions

1. Choose the antonym pair.

   a. Abundant and Scarce

   b. Several and Plenty

   c. Analysis and Review

   d. Obtrusive and Hierarchical

2. Choose the antonym pair.

   a. Bully and Animal

   b. Teary-eyed and Gentle

   c. Tough and Weak

   d. Strong and Massive

3. Choose the antonym pair.

   a. Illuminate and Obfuscate

   b. Resonance and Significance

   c. Resonate and Justify

   d. Rationalize and Practice

4. Choose the antonym pair.

   a. Simple and Complex

   b. Plain and Plaid

   c. Shy and Sinister

   d. Vibrant and Cheery

5. Choose the antonym pair.

   a. Elevate and Escalate

   b. Exhibit and Conceal

   c. Boast and Brood

   d. Show and Contest

6. Choose the antonym pair.

    a. Strict and Tight

    b. Hurtful and Offensive

    c. Unpleasant and Mean

    d. Stingy and Generous

7. Choose the antonym pair.

    a. New and Torn

    b. Advance and Retreat

    c. Next and Last

    d. Followed and Continued

8. Choose the antonym pair.

    a. Halt and Speed

    b. Began and Amidst

    c. Stop and Delay

    d. Cease and Begin

9. Choose the antonym pair.

    a. Scary and Horrific

    b. Honor and Justice

    c. Immense and Tiny

    d. Vague and Loud

10. Choose the antonym pair.

    a. Dissatisfied and Unsatisfied

    b. Disentangle and Acknowledge

    c. Discord and Harmony

    d. Fruition and Fusion

11. Choose the antonym pair.

    a. Late and Later

    b. Latter and Former

    c. Structure and Organization

    d. Latter and Rushed

12. Choose the antonym pair.

    a. Belittle and Bemuse

    b. Shrunk and Minimal

    c. Shrink and Expand

    d. Smelly and Odor

13. Choose the antonym pair.

    a. Repulsive and Repentant

    b. Reluctant and Enthusiastic

    c. Prepare and Ready

    d. Release and Give

14. Choose the antonym pair.

    a. Sovereign and Autonomy

    b. Disdain and Contempt

    c. Disorder and Disarray

    d. Refuse and Agree

15. Choose the antonym pair.

    a. Gentle and Soft

    b. Fragile and Breakable

    c. Vulnerable and Strong

    d. Vain and Tidy

16. Select the antonym of authentic.

a. Real

b. Imitation

c. Apparition

d. Dream

17. Select the antonym of villain.

a. Actor

b. Actress

c. Heroine

d. Hero

18. Select the antonym of vanish.

a. Appear

b. Lose

c. Reflection

d. Empty

19. Select the antonym of literal.

a. Manuscript

b. Writing

c. Figurative

d. Untrue

20. Select the antonym of harsh.

a. Mild

b. Light

c. Bulky

d. Bothersome

21. Select the antonym of splurge.

   a. Spend
   b. Count
   c. Use
   d. Save

22. Select the antonym of idle.

   a. Occupied
   b. Vacant
   c. Busy
   d. Interested

23. Select the antonym of console.

   a. Aggravate
   b. Empathize
   c. Sympathize
   d. Cry

24. Select the antonym of deranged.

   a. Chaos
   b. Dirty
   c. Bleak
   d. Sane

25. Select the antonym of disjointed.

   a. Connected
   b. Dismayed
   c. Recognized
   d. Bountiful

26. Select the antonym of confused.

   a. Frustrated
   b. Ashamed
   c. Enlightened
   d. Unknown

27. Select the antonym of benevolent.

   a. Nice
   b. Mature
   c. Honest
   d. Indifferent

28. Select the antonym of illicit.

   a. Unlawful
   b. Legal
   c. Anonymous
   d. Deceitful

29. Select the antonym of sterile.

   a. Dirty
   b. Alcoholic
   c. Drunk
   d. Drug

30. Select the antonym of myriad.

   a. Many
   b. Several
   c. Few
   d. Plenty

Antonyms Answer Key

1. A
Abundant and scarce are antonyms.

2. C
Tough and weak are antonyms.

3. A
Illuminate and obfuscate are antonyms.

4. A
Simple and complex are antonyms.

5. B
Exhibit and conceal are antonyms.

6. D
Stingy and generous are antonyms.

7. B
Advance and retreat are antonyms.

8. D
Cease and begin are antonyms.

9. C
Immense and tiny are antonyms.

10. C
Discord and harmony are antonyms.

11. B
Latter and former are antonyms.

12. C
Shrink and expand are antonyms.

13. B
Reluctant and enthusiastic are antonyms.

14. D
Refuse and agree are antonyms.

15. C
Vulnerable and strong are antonyms.

16. B
Authentic and imitation are antonyms.

17. D
Villain and hero are antonyms.

18. A
Vanish and appear are antonyms.

19. C
Literal and figurative are antonyms.

20. A
Harsh and mild are antonyms.

21. D
Splurge and save are antonyms.

22. C
Idle and busy are antonyms.

23. A
Console and aggravate are antonyms.

24. D
Deranged and sane are antonyms.

25. A
Disjointed and connected are antonyms.

26. C
Confused and enlightened are antonyms.

27. D
Benevolent and indifferent are antonyms.

28. B
Illicit and legal are antonyms.

29. A
Sterile and dirty are antonyms.

30. C
Myriad and few are antonyms.

How to Prepare for a Test

MOST STUDENTS HIDE THEIR HEADS AND PROCRASTINATE WHEN FACED WITH PREPARING FOR AN EXAM, HOPING THAT SOMEHOW THEY WILL BE SPARED THE AGONY, ESPECIALLY IF IT IS A BIG ONE THAT THEIR FUTURES RELY ON. Avoiding a test is what many students do best and unfortunately, they suffer the consequences because of their lack of preparation.

Test preparation requires strategy and dedication. It is the perfect training ground for a professional life. Besides having several reliable strategies, successful students also has a clear goal and know how to accomplish it. These tried and true concepts have worked well and will make your test preparation easier.

The Study Approach

Take responsibility for your own test preparation.

It is a common - but big - mistake to link your studying to someone else's. Study partners are great, but only if they are reliable. It is your job to be prepared for the test, even if a study partner fails you. Do not allow others to distract you from your goals.

Prioritize the time available to study

When do you learn best, early in the day or at night? Does your mind absorb and retain information most efficiently in small blocks of time, or do you require long stretches to get the most done? It is important to figure out the best blocks of time available to you when you can be the most productive. Try to consolidate activities to allow for longer periods of study time.

Find a quiet place where you will not be disturbed

Do not try to squeeze in quality study time in any old location. Find a quiet place with a minimum of distractions, such as the library, a park or even the laundry room. Good lighting is essential and you need to have comfortable seating and a desk surface large enough to hold your materials. It is probably not a great idea to study in your bedroom. You might be distracted by clothes on the floor, a book you have been planning to read, the telephone or something else. Besides, in the middle of studying, that bed will start to look very comfortable. Whatever you do, avoid using the bed as a place to study since you might fall asleep to avoiding studying!

The exception is flashcards. By far the most productive study time is sitting down and studying and studying only. However, with flashcards you can carry them with you and make use of odd moments, like standing in line or waiting for the bus. This isn't as productive, but it really helps and is definitely worth doing.

Determine what you need to study

Gather together your books, your notes, your laptop and any other materials needed to focus on your study for this exam. Ensure you have everything you need so you don't waste time. Remember paper, pencils and erasers, sticky notes, bottled water and a snack. Keep your phone with you if you need it to find essential information, but keep it turned off so others can't distract you.

Have a positive attitude

It is essential that you approach your studies for the test with an attitude that says you will pass it. And pass it with flying colors! This is one of the most important keys to successful studying. Believing that you are capable helps you to become capable.

The Strategy of Studying

Review class notes

Stay on top of class notes and assignments by reviewing them frequently and regularly and regularly. Re-writing notes can be a terrific study trick, as it helps lock in information. Pay special attention to any comments that have been made by the teacher. If a study guide has been made available as part of the class materials, use it! It will be a valuable tool to use for studying.

Estimate how much time you will need

If you are concerned about the time you have available it is a good idea to set up a schedule so that you do not get bogged down on one section and end without enough time left to study other things. Remember to schedule breaks, and use that time for a little exercise or other stress reducing techniques.

Test yourself to determine your weaknesses

Look online for additional assessment and evaluation tools available like practice questions for a particular subject. Visit our website https://www.test-preparation.ca for test tips and more practice questions. Once you have determined your weaknesses, you can focus on these, and just brush up on the other areas of the exam.

Mental Prep – How to Psych Yourself Up for a Test

Since tests are often a big factor in your final grade or acceptance into a program, it is understandable that taking tests can create a great deal of anxiety for many students. Even students who know they have learned the required material find their minds going blank as they stare at the test booklet. You can avoid test anxiety by preparing yourself mentally. One easy way to overcome that anxiety is to prepare mentally for the test with a few simple techniques. **Do not procrastinate**

Study the material for the test when it becomes available, and continue to review the material until the test day. By waiting until the last minute and trying to cram for the test the night before, you actually increase anxiety. This leads to negative self-talk, which becomes self-fulfilling. Telling yourself "I can't learn this. I am going to fail" is a pretty sure indication that you are right.

Positive self-talk.

Positive self-talk drowns out negative self-talk and to increases your confidence level. Whenever you begin feeling overwhelmed or anxious about the test, remind yourself that you have studied enough, you know the material and that you will pass the test. Both negative and positive self-talk are really just your fantasy, so why not choose to be a winner?

Do not compare yourself to others.

Do not compare yourself to other students. Instead, focus on your strengths and weaknesses and prepare accordingly. Regardless of how others perform, your performance is the only one that matters to your grade. Comparing yourself to others increases your anxiety and negative self-talk before the test.

Visualize.

Make a mental image of yourself taking the test. You know the answers and feel relaxed. Visualize doing well on the test and having no problems with the material. Visualizations can increase your confidence and decrease the anxiety you might otherwise feel before the test. Instead of thinking of this as a test, see it as an opportunity to demonstrate what you have learned!

Avoid negativity.

Worry is contagious and viral - once it gets started it builds on itself. Cut it off before it gets to be a problem. Even if you are relaxed and confident, being around anxious, worried classmates might cause you to start feeling anxious. Before the test, tune out the fears of classmates. Feeling anxious and worried before an exam is normal, and every student experiences those feelings at some point. But you cannot allow these feelings to interfere with your performance. Practicing mental preparation techniques and remembering that the test is not the only measure of your academic performance will ease your anxiety and ensure that you perform at your best.

How to Take a Test

EVERYONE KNOWS THAT TAKING AN EXAM IS STRESSFUL, BUT IT DOES NOT HAVE TO BE THAT BAD! There are a few simple things that you can do to increase your score on any type of test. Take a look at these tips and consider how you can incorporate them into your study time.

OK - so you are in the test room - Here is what to do!

Reading the Instructions

This is the most basic point, but one that, surprisingly, many students ignore and it costs big time! Since reading the instructions is one of the most common, and 100% preventable mistakes, we have a whole section just on reading instructions.

Pay close attention to the sample questions. Almost all standardized tests offer sample questions, paired with their correct solutions. Go through these to make sure that you understand what they mean and how they arrived at the correct answer. Do not be afraid to ask the test supervisor for help with a sample that confuses you, or instructions that you are unsure of.

Tips for Reading the Question

We could write pages and pages of tips just on reading the test questions. Here are a few that will help you the most.

- **Think first.** Before you look at the answer, read and think about the question. It is best to try to come up with the correct answer before you look at the options. This way, when the test-writer tries to trick you with a close answer, you will not fall for it.

- **Make it true or false.** If a question confuses you,

then look at each answer option and think of it as a "true" "false" question. Select the one that seems most likely to be "true."

- **Mark the Question.** Don't be afraid to mark up the test booklet. Unless you are specifically told not to mark in the booklet, use it to your advantage.

- **Circle Key Words.** As you are reading the question, underline or circle key words. This helps you to focus on the most critical information needed to solve the problem. For example, if the question said, "Which of these is not a synonym for huge?" You might circle "not," "synonym" and "huge." That clears away the clutter and lets you focus on what is important.

- **Always underline these words:** all, none, always, never, most, best, true, false and except.

- **Eliminate.** Elimination is the best strategy for multiple choice answers *and* questions. If you are confused by lengthy questions, cross out anything that you think is irrelevant, obviously wrong, or information that you think is offered to distract you. Elimination is the most valuable strategy!

- **Do not try to read between the lines.** Usually, questions are written to be straightforward, with no deep, underlying meaning. Generally, the simple answer really is the correct answer. Do not over-analyze!

How to Take a Test - The Basics

Some sections of the test are designed to assess your ability to quickly grab the necessary information; this type of exam makes speed a priority. Others are more concerned with your depth of knowledge, and how accurate it is. When you start a new section of the test, look it over to determine whether the test is for speed or accuracy. If the test is for speed (a lot of questions and a short time), your strategy is clear; answer as many questions as quickly as possible.

The PSB does NOT penalize for wrong answers, so if all else fails, guess and make sure you answer every question.

Every little bit helps

The PSB does NOT allow personal calculators. You cannot bring any other materials into the test room. Scratch paper and a pencil are provided. Use them!

Make time your friend

Budget your time from the beginning until you are finished, and stick to it! The time for each section will be included in the instructions.

Easy does it

One smart way to tackle a test is to locate the easy questions and answer those first. This is a time-tested strategy that never fails, because it saves you a lot of unnecessary anxiety. First, read the question and decide if you can answer it in less than a minute. If so, complete the question and go to the next one. If not, skip it for now and continue to the next question. By the time you have completed the first pass through this section of the exam, you will have answered a good number of questions. Not only does it boost your confidence, relieve anxiety and kick your memory up a notch, you will know exactly how many questions remain and can allot the rest of your time accordingly. Think of doing the easy questions first as a warm-up!

Do not watch your watch

At best, taking an important exam is an uncomfortable situation. If you are like most people, you might be tempted to subconsciously distract yourself from the task at hand. One of the most common ways is by becoming obsessed with your watch or the wall clock. Do not watch your watch! Take it off and place it on the top corner of your desk, far enough away that you will not be tempted to look at it every two minutes. Better still, turn the watch face away from you. That way, every time you try to sneak a peek, you will be reminded to refocus your attention to the task at hand. Give yourself permission to check your watch or the wall clock after you complete each section. Focus on answering the questions, not on how many minutes have elapsed since you last looked at it.

Divide and conquer

What should you do when you come across a question that is so complicated you may not even be certain what is being asked? As we have suggested, the first time through, skip the question. At some point, you will need to return to it and get it under control. The best way to handle questions that leave you feeling so anxious you can hardly think is by breaking them into manageable pieces. Solving smaller bits is always easier. For complicated questions, divide them into bite-sized pieces and solve these smaller sets separately. Once you understand what the reduced sections are really saying, it will be much easier to put them together and get a handle on the bigger question. This may not work with every question - see below for how to deal with questions you cannot break down.

Reason your way through the toughest questions

If you find that a question is so dense you can't figure out how to break it into smaller pieces, there are a few strategies that might help. First, read the question again and look for hints. Can you re-word the question in one or more different ways? This may give you clues. Look for words that can function as either verbs or nouns, and try to figure out what the questions is asking from the sentence structure. Remember that many nouns in English have several different meanings. While some of those meanings might be related, sometimes they are completely distinct. If reading the sentence one way does not make sense, consider a different definition or meaning for a key word.

The truth is, it is not always necessary to understand a question to arrive at a correct answer! The most successful strategy for multiple choice is Elimination. Frequently, at least one answer is clearly wrong and can be crossed off the list of possible correct answers. Next, look at the remaining answers and eliminate any that are only partially true. You may still have to flat-out guess from time to time, but using the process of elimination will help you make your way to the correct answer more often than not - even when you don't know what the question means!

Do not leave early

Use all the time allotted to you, even if you can't wait to get out of the testing room. Instead, once you have finished, spend the remaining time reviewing your answers. Go back to those questions that were most difficult for you and review your response. Another good way to use this time is to return to multiple-choice questions in which you filled in a bubble. Do a spot check, reviewing every fifth or sixth question to make sure your answer coincides with the bubble you filled in. This is a great way to catch yourself if you made a mistake, skipped a bubble and therefore put all your answers in the wrong bubbles!

Become a super sleuth and look for careless errors. Look for questions that have double negatives or other odd phrasing; they might be an attempt to throw you off. Careless errors on your part might be the result of skimming a question and missing a key word. Words such as "always," "never," "sometimes," "rarely" and the like can give a strong indication of the answer the question is really seeking. Don't throw away points by being careless!

Just as you budgeted time at the beginning of the test to allow for easy and more difficult questions, be sure to budget sufficient time to review your answers. On essay questions and math questions where you are required to show your work, check your writing to make sure it is legible.

Math questions can be especially tricky. The best way to double check math questions is by figuring the answer using a different method, if possible.

Here is another terrific tip. It is likely that no matter how hard you try, you will have a handful of questions you just are not sure of. Keep them in mind as you read through the rest of the test. If you can't answer a question, looking back over the test to find a different question that addresses the same topic might give you clues.

We know that taking the test has been stressful and you can hardly wait to escape. Leaving before you double-check as much as possible can be a quick trip to disaster. Taking a few extra minutes can make the difference between getting a bad grade and a great one. Besides, there will be lots of time to relax and celebrate after the test is turned in.

In the Test Room – What you MUST do!

If you are like the rest of the world, there is almost nothing you would rather avoid than taking a test. Unfortunately, that is not an option if you want to pass. Rather than suffer, consider a few attitude adjustments that might turn the experience from a horrible one to...well, an interesting one! Take a look at these tips. Simply changing how you perceive the experience can change the experience itself.

You have to take the test - you can't change that. What you can change, and the only thing that you can change, is your attitude -so get a grip - you can do it!

Get in the mood

After weeks of studying, the big day has finally arrived. The worst thing you can do is arrive at the test site feeling frustrated, worried, and anxious. Keep a check on your emotional state. If your emotions are shaky before a test it can determine how well you do on the test. It is extremely important that you pump yourself up, believe in yourself, and use that confidence to get in the mood!

Don't fight reality

Students often resent tests, and with good reason. After all, many people do not test well, and they know the grade they end with does not accurately reflect their true knowledge. It is easy to feel resentful because tests classify students and create categories that just don't seem fair. Face it: Students who are great at rote memorization and not that good at actually analyzing material often score higher than those who might be more creative thinkers and balk at simply memorizing cold, hard facts. It may not be fair, but there it is anyway. Conformity is an asset on tests, and creativity is often a liability. There is no point in wasting time or energy being upset about this reality. The first step is to accept the reality and get used to it. You will get higher marks when you realize tests do count and that you must give them your best effort. Think about your future and the career that is easier to achieve if you have consistently earned high grades. Avoid negative energy and focus on anything that lifts your enthusiasm and increases your motivation.

Get there early enough to relax

If you are tense, scared, anxious, or feeling rushed, it will cost you. Get to the exam room early and relax before you go in. This way, when the exam starts, you are comfortable and ready to apply yourself. Of course, you do not want to arrive so early that you are the only one there. That will not help you relax; it will only give you too much time to sit there, worry and get wound up all over again.

If you can, visit the room where you will be taking your exam a few days ahead of time. Having a visual image of the room can be surprisingly calming, because it takes away one of the big 'unknowns'. Not only that, but once you have visited, you know how to get there and will not be worried about getting lost. Furthermore, driving to the test site once lets you know how much time you need to allow for the trip. That means three potential stressors have been eliminated all at once.

Get it down on paper

One advantage of arriving early is that it allows you time to recreate notes. If you spend a lot of time worrying about whether you will be able to remember information like names, dates, places, and mathematical formulas, there is a solution for that. Unless the exam you are taking allows you to use your books and notes, (and very few do) you will have to rely on memory. Arriving early gives to time to tap into your memory and jot down key pieces of information you know that will be asked. Just make certain you are allowed to make notes once you are in the testing site; not all locations will permit it. Once you get your test, on a small piece of paper write down everything you are afraid you will forget. It will take a minute or two but by dumping your worries onto the page you have effectively eliminated anxiety and driven off the panic you feel.

Get comfortable in your chair

Here is a clever technique that releases physical stress and helps you get comfortable, even relaxed in your body. You will tense and hold each of your muscles for just a few seconds. The trick is, you must tense them hard for the technique to work. You might want to practice this technique a few times at home; you do not want an unfamiliar technique to add to your stress just before a test, after all! Once you are at the test site, this exercise can always be done in the rest room or another quiet location.

Start with the muscles in your face then work down your body. Tense, squeeze and hold the muscles for a moment or two. Notice the feel of every muscle as you go down your body. Scowl to tense your forehead, pull in your chin to tense your neck. Squeeze your shoulders down to tense your back. Pull in your stomach all the way back to your ribs, make your lower back tight then stretch your fingers. Tense your leg muscles and calves then stretch your feet and your toes. You should be as stiff as a board throughout your entire body.

Now relax your muscles in reverse starting with your toes. Notice how all the muscles feel as you relax them one by one. Once you have released a muscle or set of muscles, allow them to remain relaxed as you proceed up your body. Focus on how you are feeling as all the tension leaves. Start breathing deeply when you get to your chest muscles. By the time you have found your chair, you will be so relaxed it will feel like bliss!

Fight distraction

A lucky few are able to focus deeply when taking an important examination, but most people are easily distracted, probably because they would rather be any place else! There are several things you can do to protect yourself from distraction.

Stay away from windows.

If you sit near a window you are adding an unnecessary distraction.

Choose a seat away from the aisle so you do not become distracted by people who leave early. People who leave the exam room early are often the ones who fail. Do not compare your time to theirs.

Of course, you love your friends; that's why they are your friends! In the test room, however, they should become complete strangers inside your mind. Forget they are there. The first step is to distance yourself physically from friends or classmates. That way, you will not be tempted to glance at them to see how they are doing, and there will be no chance of eye contact that could either distract you or even lead to an accusation of cheating. Furthermore, if they are feeling stressed because they did not spend the focused time studying that you did, their anxiety is less likely to permeate your hard-earned calm.

Of course, you will want to choose a seat where there is sufficient light. Nothing is worse than trying to take an important examination under flickering lights or dim bulbs.

Ask the instructor or exam proctor to close the door if there is a lot of noise outside. If the instructor or proctor is unable to do so, block out the noise as best you can. Do not let anything disturb you.

The PSB does not allow any personal items in the exam room. Eat protein, complex carbohydrates and a little fat to keep you feeling full and to supercharge your energy. Nothing is worse than a sudden drop in blood sugar during an exam.

Do not allow yourself to become distracted by being too cold or hot. Regardless of the weather outside, carry a sweater, scarf or jacket if the air conditioning at the test site is set too high, or the heat set too low. By the same token, dress in layers so that you are prepared for a range of temperatures.

Watch Caffeine

Drinking a gallon of coffee or gulping a few energy drinks might seem like a great idea, but it is, in fact, a very bad one. Caffeine, pep pills or other artificial sources of energy are more likely to leave you feeling rushed and ragged. Your brain might be clicking along, all right, but chances are good it is not clicking along on the right track! Furthermore, drinking coffee or energy drinks will mean frequent trips to the rest room. This will cut into the time you should be spending answering questions and is a distraction in itself, since each time you need to leave the room you lose focus. Pep pills will only make it harder to think clearly when solving complicated problems.

At the same time, if anxiety is your problem try to find ways around using tranquilizers during test-taking time. Even medically prescribed anti-anxiety medication can make you less alert and even decrease your motivation. Motivation is what you need to get you through an exam. If your anxiety is so bad that it threatens to interfere with your ability to take an exam, speak to your doctor and ask for documentation. Many testing sites will allow non-distracting test rooms, extended testing time and other accommodations with a doctor's note that explains the situation is made available.

Keep Breathing

It might not make a lot of sense, but when people become anxious, tense, or scared, their breathing becomes shallow and, sometimes stop breathing all together! Pay attention to your emotions, and when you are feeling worried, focus on your breathing. Take a moment to remind yourself to breathe deeply and regularly. Drawing in steady, deep breaths energizes the body. When you continue to breathe deeply you will notice you exhale all the tension.

If you feel you need to, try rehearsing breathing at home. With continued practice of this relaxation technique, you will begin to know the muscles that tense up under pressure. Call these your "signal muscles." These are the ones that will speak to you first, begging you to relax. Take the time to listen to those muscles and do as they ask. With just a little breathing practice, you will get into the habit of checking yourself regularly and when you realize you are tense, relaxation will become second nature.

Common Test-Taking Mistakes

Taking a test is not much fun at best. When you take a test and make a stupid mistake that affects your grade negatively, it is natural to be upset, especially when it is something that could have been easily avoided. So what are some of the common mistakes that are made on tests?

Put your name on the test!

How could you possibly forget to put your name on a test? You would be amazed at how often that happens. Very often, tests without names are thrown out immediately, resulting in a failing grade.

Marking the wrong multiple-choice answer

It is important to work at a steady pace, but that does not mean bolting through the questions. Be sure the answer you are marking is the one you mean to. If the bubble you need to fill in or the answer you need to circle is 'C', do not allow yourself to get distracted and select 'B' instead.

Answering a question twice

Some multiple-choice test questions have two very similar

answers. If you are in too much of a hurry, you might select them both. Remember that only one answer is correct, so if you choose more than one, you have automatically failed that question.

Mishandling a difficult question

We recommend skipping difficult questions and returning to them later, but beware! First, be certain that you do return to the question. Circling the entire passage or placing a large question mark beside it will help you spot it when you are reviewing your test. Secondly, if you are not careful to skip the question, you can mess yourself up badly. Imagine that a question is too difficult and you decide to save it for later. You read the next question, which you know the answer to, and you fill in that answer. You continue to the end of the test then return to the difficult question only to discover you didn't actually skip it! Instead, you inserted the answer to the following question in the spot reserved for the harder one, thus throwing off the remainder of your test!

Incorrectly Transferring an answer from scratch paper

This can happen easily if you are trying to hurry! Double check any answer you have figured out on scratch paper, and make sure what you have written on the test itself is an exact match!

Thinking too much

Generally, your first thought is your best thought. If you worry yourself into insecurity, your self-doubts can trick you into choosing an incorrect answer when your first impulse was the right one!

Conclusion

CONGRATULATIONS! You have made it this far because you have applied yourself diligently to practicing for the exam and no doubt improved your potential score considerably! Passing your up-coming exam is a huge step in a journey that might be challenging at times but will be many times more rewarding and fulfilling. That is why being prepared is so important.

Study then Practice and then Succeed!

Good Luck!

Visit Us Online

Taking a test? We can help!

Complete study guides, practice test questions, study tips and more:

www.test-preparation.ca

https://www.facebook.com/CompleteTestPreparation/

https://www.youtube.com/user/MrTestPreparation

https://www.instagram.com/completetestpreparation/

https://www.pinterest.ca/brians6634/boards/

Online Resources

How to Prepare for a Test - The Ultimate Guide

https://www.test-preparation.ca/the-ultimate-guide-to-test-preparation-strategy/

Learning Styles - The Complete Guide

https://www.test-preparation.ca/learning-styles/

Test Anxiety Secrets!

https://www.test-preparation.ca/how-to-overcome-test-anxiety/

Time Management on a Test

https://www.test-preparation.ca/test-tactics-the-time-wise-approach/

Flash Cards - The Complete Guide

https://www.test-preparation.ca/test-preparation-with-flash-cards/

Test Preparation Video Series

https://www.test-preparation.ca/video-series-on-test-preparation-multiple-choice-strategies-and-how-to-study/

How to Memorize - The Complete Guide

https://www.test-preparation.ca/a-guide-to-memorizing-anything-easily-and-painlessly/

www.ingramcontent.com/pod-product-compliance
Lightning Source LLC
Chambersburg PA
CBHW071826080526
44589CB00012B/932